HOW THE COURTS WORK

HOW THE COURTS WORK

A Plain English Explanation of the American Legal System

By

Marilyn Englander & Curtis Karnow

VANDEPLAS PUBLISHING

UNITED STATES OF AMERICA

How the courts work
A plain english explanation of the american legal system

Englander, Marilyn & Karnow, Curtis

Published by:

Vandeplas Publishing - October 2008

801 International Parkway, 5th Floor
Lake Mary, FL. 32746
USA

www.vandeplaspublishing.com

ISBN: 978-1-60042-055-9

With gratitude to our parents

And hope for our children

Table of Contents

Foreword..1
  Chapter 1: A Typical Case 3
    Summary of the Cases 3
  Chapter 2: Introduction 9
    "A nation of laws, not of men"..9
    Who says what the law is 10
    Juries and judges: facts and law...11
    The U.S. Constitution and the Supremacy Clause 13
  Chapter 3: The State and the Federal Governments....................15
    Federal Responsibilities..15
    State Responsibilities 16
  Chapter 4: The Three Branches 17
    Legislative...17
    Executive...17
    Judicial..18
  Chapter 5: How the Judicial system is organized 21
    Federal system...21
      Bankruptcy judges...22
      U.S. magistrate judges..22
      Federal district (trial) courts 23
      Circuit Courts of Appeals 25
      U.S. Supreme Court..26
    State System 28
      State Supreme Court...30
      Courts of Appeal 30
      Superior Courts..31
  Chapter 6: Criminal Law vs. Civil Law..33
    Criminal Cases..34
      Constitutional Rights...35
        The Fourth Amendment (protection from unreasonable search & seizure)....................................35
        The Fifth Amendment ("right not to incriminate oneself," also known as *Miranda* rights") 37
        The Sixth Amendment ("right to a lawyer" or *Gideon*)........38
        The Sixth Amendment ("right to a jury") 38
      Waiving or giving up rights..39
    Civil Cases...39
  Chapter 7: Introduction to the Hierarchy of Law.......................45

Chapter 8: Federal Law 47
  The Constitution...47
  Federal Treaties 47
  Federal Statutes..48
Chapter 9: State Law..49
Chapter 10: Decisional Law 51
Chapter 11: Judges...55
  What Judges Do...56
  How Judges Get the Job..58
  Constraints on the Power of Judges 61
Chapter 12: A Story about a Civil Case 69
  The Complaint is Filed 70
  The Role of Insurance...71
  The Answer is Filed 71
  Motion to Dismiss, and Demurrer..72
  Discovery 73
    Interrogatories 74
    Requests for Admission...75
    Depositions..75
    Document Demands 76
    Objections 77
  Motion for Summary Judgment...78
  Settlement and Settlement Conferences 79
  Getting Ready for Trial...81
  Trial..82
    The Burden of Proof: By a Preponderance of the Evidence........82
    Judge ("Bench") vs. Jury Trial 82
    Getting Called for Jury Service...83
    Jury Selection 84
    Opening Statements...87
    Plaintiff's Evidence..88
    Motion for Directed Verdict..91
    Defendant's Evidence...93
    Rebuttal...93
    Jury Instructions..93
    Closing Arguments 94
    Jury Deliberations..96
    Verdict...97
  Appeal to the Court of Appeal 100
  Filing Certiorari Petition to the Supreme Court 104
  Executing on the Judgment...104

Chapter 13: A Story about a Criminal Case 107
   Infractions vs. Misdemeanors vs. Felonies 110
      Probable Cause and the Role of the Grand Jury 110
   Motion to Suppress 112
   Pretrial Discussions and Settlement Explorations 114
   Discovery 115
      Statutory Rights 116
      Constitutional Rights (due process) - Exculpatory Evidence ... 116
   Trial 117
      Jury Selection 118
      Opening Statements 120
      People's Evidence 121
      Motion for Acquittal 124
      Defendant's Case 125
      Rebuttal 125
      Jury Instructions & Closing Argument 126
      Jury Deliberations 127
      Verdict 128
      Sentencing 130
      Appeals 133
      Revocation of Probation 134
Conclusion 137
About the Authors 139
Appendices 141
   Map of a courtroom 142
   Federal court system 143
   California state court system 144
   Sample criminal code excerpts 145
   Sample court memorandum & order 148
   Sample court minutes of a sentencing 151
   Resources 153

x

Foreword

Citizens are generally unaware of who their judges are, what sort of work judges do, what happens at a trial or why it happens. Those who report for jury duty have no sense of how a trial progresses nor what their role, as jurors, involves. Few understand how the case got to trial in the first place. Non-lawyers are intimidated by legal terms, which include words from Latin and old English, not to speak of the plethora of acronyms. Many people are alienated from the court system, reluctant to perform jury duty, and sometimes (through their ignorance) they fear legal procedure.

Indeed, even newly minted lawyers usually have no overall sense of how a case progresses through the courts. In law school they were taught specific substantive law such as contracts, torts, administrative law and criminal law, but they possess little practical understanding of the workings of the legal system.

Yet our legal system, with its foundations in the U.S. Constitution, is an extraordinary achievement, envied by others across the world who cannot rely on an independent judiciary or even basic fairness and transparency in their court systems. The U.S. legal system is a treasure beyond reckoning.

To preserve our treasure, however, we must understand it. We must know what we have. When the judiciary comes under partisan attack, or when public clamor over a particular court result threatens the underlying principle of an independent judiciary, the debate turns to chaos when it is fed by ignorance. Only if citizens have a basic legal literacy can we hope to preserve our system --- a government of laws, and not of men --- that our predecessors fought so hard to create.

This book's goal is to improve the reader's legal literacy. It introduces and defines basic legal terms. The book maps out all the stages in both a civil and a criminal case. It does this by telling a fictionalized story of two related "drunk driving" cases. The driver accused of "driving under the influence" is prosecuted by the district attorney in a criminal case. And he is the subject of a civil case brought by the victims, the people in the car he hit. As our stories progress, the reader will come to understand the role of all the main participants in a trial, the differences between federal and state cases, how appeals work, what judges do, what jurors do and the guiding role of the U.S. Constitution.

In the next section, we introduce the basic story in shortened form, and then revisit the civil and criminal narratives in detail later in the book. The stories presented here are fiction, and often are exaggerated for the sake of emphasis and dramatic flair. The names of the judges and lawyers are borrowed from friends of the authors, but the characters in this book bear no relationship to those people or anyone else. Nothing here is a comment or reflection on any real proceeding, and nothing here indicates what any judge, including one of the authors here, would do in a real case.

Chapter 1: A Typical Case

The first time a person confronts the judicial system, it is confusing. The procedures, and the reasons for them, are unclear. Words are unrecognizable. A person may have no sense of the steps each case typically goes through. In the next section, we briefly describe a typical, if fictive, case. At first, the reader may not follow every step described in this next section, but each will be explained later in this book.

Summary of the Cases

On the evening of June 25, 2006, Ervin Johnson sat in his local bar. By eleven P.M., he had consumed ten beers. He staggered off his bar stool and waggling his car keys in his hand, waved goodbye to Ed, the bartender. He lurched out the door and into the warm night, got into his pickup truck and drove away. Five minutes later he went through a red light and hit a car broadside. The passenger of the sedan, Kim Hollings, was killed outright, while the car's driver, her friend Harry Pitt, was seriously injured. (He was to spend months in the hospital recovering, and lost his right arm as a result. He also missed six months at his job.)

After the police arrived at the scene, they arrested Johnson. He spent two days in the county hospital for minor injuries, in a special section set aside for prisoners, and then was taken to court in connection with the criminal case against him.

Two cases were filed in state court as a result of this tragedy. The first was a criminal case, a case titled *People v. Ervin Johnson*. The "People" of the state, represented by the local district attorney, who was the prosecutor in the case, filed charges of second degree murder, driving while under the influence, and some other criminal charges. The prosecutor was hoping Johnson would eventually get a sentence of about

20 years in state prison. The trial in this first case was in front of a judge in the state court's criminal division.

A month later, a civil case was filed against Johnson. This law suit was brought by Harry Pitt, and by the parents of Kim Hollings on behalf of their dead daughter. This wrongful death civil case asked for money damages against Johnson; specifically, the complaint in this case asked for a total of ten million dollars. The complaint—the complaint is the first paper filed in a civil case, and sets out a brief summary of why the person who brings the case is entitled to money—asked for one million dollars in compensatory damages. The one million dollars was for the medical treatments Harry Pitt would need for the rest of his life. The complaint also asked for compensation for lost earnings, plus three million dollars for "pain and suffering." This was to compensate Kim and Harry for the pain and suffering they had and Pitt would in the future endure. In addition, the complaint asked for six million dollars in punitive damages. This was to punish Ervin Johnson for the outrageous nature of his act of driving drunk and killing Hollings. This civil case was titled *H. Pitt and K. Hollings vs. Ervin Johnson.*

Johnson did not have to pay for his lawyer in the civil case, because his car insurance company provided a lawyer. He also needed a lawyer in his criminal case, but couldn't afford it. Because it was a criminal case, he got the court to appoint a lawyer for him, free of charge, from the public defender's office.

As it turned out, Hollings and Pitt didn't have to pay any money for their lawyer in the civil case, either. That was because, in this case, the lawyer (named Don Simon) agreed to take the case without charging anything in advance: Don Simon would, if the case were successful, take one third of the total money obtained from the jury verdict. If Hollings and Pitt lost the case, they, and their lawyer Simon, would get nothing. Simon was willing to take the civil case on these terms, known as a *contingency agreement*, because he was confident that he would win the case.

The Criminal Case

Here's what happened in the criminal case, *People v. Johnson.* The prosecutor—the assistant direct attorney assigned to the case—offered to settle the case for fifteen years in state prison if Johnson would plead guilty. This was the "deal," a plea bargain, that the prosecutor offered, in return for not having to take the case to trial. But Johnson turned down the offer. He wanted a jury trial, hoping that the prosecutor might not be able to persuade a jury that he, Johnson, had really been "under the influence" of alcohol (DUI). Johnson also hoped that the jury might think the other car—the sedan driven by Hollings and Pitt—had been responsible for the accident, or at least that the jury might have enough doubts not to convict. As his lawyer told Johnson, even if one juror had a reasonable doubt, there could be no conviction, and the prosecutor might later offer a better deal if and when the jury was unable to come to an unanimous verdict. Johnson's lawyer asked the prosecutor to agree to a three year jail sentence. The assistant district attorney refused that deal, and insisted on fifteen years. Five months later, the case went to trial. They picked a jury, had opening statements, and called witnesses.

After the evidence, the judge spent about twenty minutes telling the jury what the law was, discussing the definition of "reasonable doubt", "second degree murder", and the definition of lesser offenses, or less serious crimes, that the jury might find Johnson guilty of. The jury was then taken to the jury room. There, they deliberated for a few days. The jury had to be unanimous, and find the People had proved their case "beyond a reasonable doubt" before they could convict. In the end they found Johnson guilty of second degree murder. They also found him guilty of aggravated battery because of the injuries inflicted on Pitt, and of driving under the influence of alcohol.

The judge ordered a pre-sentence report from the probation department on Johnson. This report reviewed his prior criminal record, provided a lot of information about his background, and contained a recommendation on the sentence. Because he had prior convictions for drunk driving, the probation department recommended the maximum term in prison for the charge, 20 years in state prison. The judge agreed, and sentenced Johnson to 20 years, plus an additional sentence of three years for the aggravated battery against Pitt. Over the next two years, the appellate court heard Johnson's appeal but the appellate court refused to overturn the conviction. The appeals court affirmed the judgment of conviction, finding that while the trial judge had made some mistakes in the case, none of them could possibly have affected the outcome of the case, and that the trial had been fair.

Johnson's lawyer filed a legal paper called a *writ* with the state supreme court, asking for a review of the decision of the court of appeal. But the Supreme Court saw no reason to take the case, and denied the writ without deciding one way or the other any of the issues in the case. That left the appellate court's opinion, which had affirmed the trial court's judgment of conviction, intact. So Johnson went on to serve out the rest of his prison sentence.

The Civil Case

Here's what happened in Johnson's civil trial, the case brought by Hollings and Pitt for a money recovery.

Hollings and Pitt used the same lawyer to file their civil complaint, that is, to sue Johnson. The lawyer, named Don Simon, filed his complaint and immediately wrote a letter to Johnson's lawyer asking for ten million dollars. There was no response. Within two weeks, Johnson's lawyer had sent Simon about a hundred pages of demands for documents. He requested reports on the medical treatment for Pitt and answers to hundreds of questions designed to see what sort of evidence Simon had against Johnson. Simon sent a similar series of questions, and demands for documents, to Johnson's lawyer. The lawyers had multiple disputes about the extent to which they really needed to answer all the questions, and whether the demands for documents were in fact overbroad and burdensome. Each accused the other of purposefully burdening the other with these demands. They took these disputes to court, and the judge ruled in each case on the extent to which the materials demanded really had to be provided to the other side.

Nine months later, Johnson's lawyer filed a motion for summary judgment. In that motion, she argued that Simon didn't have enough evidence to go to trial, and that the judge should rule in Johnson's favor right away. There were solely legal issues left in the case, Johnson's lawyer argued, and the judge could decide those now without having to have a jury trial. The judge denied the motion, and wrote an opinion in which the judge said the issues were factual, not about the law, and that they were for a jury to resolve at trial. Judges decide legal issues, and juries usually decide what the facts are. The judge then set a trial date for three months later.

Johnson's lawyer then demanded to take the sworn statement, or deposition, of Pitt. For over two days, Pitt sat in a lawyer's conference room and answered questions from Johnson's lawyer. The whole thing was video-taped, so that the important parts could be played back at trial.

Simon also wanted to take the deposition of Johnson. But Johnson objected. He said that while in the usual civil case such a deposition was of course proper, here his statement might be used against him in his criminal trial: that would interfere with his Fifth Amendment right not to testify. In fact, he said he would invoke his Fifth Amendment right not to testify if the deposition went forward, because his responses might incriminate him. He refused to answer any questions at deposition or at any civil trial. The judge agreed, and delayed the civil case until after the criminal case was complete. Unfortunately, with all the appeals in the criminal case, the delay in this civil case turned out to last about three years.

After Johnson was convicted in his criminal case, and exhausted his appeals, he was sent to prison. Then his civil case was able to proceed.

Three years after the civil case was filed, the parties went to trial. Both sides presented evidence. The judge instructed the jury on the law. The jury in this case was unable to reach a unanimous verdict, but since this was a civil case, that didn't matter. Nine out of twelve jurors was enough for a verdict. The jury actually voted 10 to 2 in favor of the plaintiffs Pitt and Hollings and against the defendant Johnson. They awarded six million dollars to compensate the plaintiffs Hollings and Pitt for their pain and suffering and medical expenses and lost income. They awarded another million dollars in punitive damages.

The case went up on appeal. Simon knew the appeal would take about two years, so he settled the seven million dollar verdict for five million dollars, and the appeal was dismissed. Johnson actually had no money, but because he was insured with high policy limits, the insurance company paid the settlement.

Simon took his one third of the recovery, about $1.6 million, and the rest went to Pitt and the family of Hollings.

By the time you finish this book, you will understand every step these cases took. You will understand the meanings of the legal terms used, which decisions in a case are made by lawyers, which by juries, and which by judges; and you will know how lawyers and judges do their job.

You will understand the legal system from the inside.

Chapter 2: Introduction

"A nation of laws, not of men"

There is much we take for granted in the United States. We generally assume that governors of states, and the President of the United States, can't simply jail anyone they want to, wherever or for as long as they like. We assume that trials and the judicial system are usually fair, that people have a chance to be heard, and that no one is above the law. We assume everyone, and every company, generally has to follow the same rules, and that if they don't, they are likely to get caught and may be sued by those they injure. We assume that when judges make their decisions, they don't just do what feels good to them personally: judges try to figure out what the law requires, and then make decisions according to the law. We assume the judge will follow the law, whether he likes the defendant or not, and irrespective of race or ethnicity issues, and that the law, whether it's in statute books or described in opinions by other judges, is equally available to anyone who wants to know about it. We assume that judges will explain why they are doing what they do, and that court proceedings will be out in the open, for anyone in the public, including the press, to watch, and that no one will be punished for making comments or criticism, or debating the issues, or urging changes.

This is what we mean when we say we're not a government of men and women, but of laws. In past times, and throughout most of the world today, "law" has been and is fickle, unpredictable, and is often made up by rulers as they go along, to suit their own purposes. In many places, the criminal and civil justice systems have been either not available at all, or they are secret, arbitrary, and unresponsive to the people who live under their yoke. It is not justice by any definition.

Here's a compelling example of how justice works in the United States. A subpoena is a type of court order. Subpoenas require that things (like papers) or people show up at a certain time and place, generally in court. No one is exempt from court subpoenas. No one is immune. In 1973 a trial judge in Washington D.C. ordered President Richard M. Nixon to produce tape recordings he had secretly made in the White House. The President refused. President Nixon wrote to the judge, "I must decline to obey the command of that subpoena. In so doing I follow the example of a long line of my predecessors who have consistently adhered to the position that the president is not subject to compulsory process from the courts...." The President then appealed the trial judge's order and subpoena all the way to the U.S. Supreme Court. The Supreme Court ordered the President to comply with the trial court's order. He finally complied, and turned over all the tapes. Later President Nixon resigned, in part because of the criminal actions that those tapes revealed.

No one is above the law.

Who says what the law is

Who says what the law is? Before we answer that question, it's helpful to understand that there are three general ways in which law is made. First, the people of this nation have embraced a constitution, which is changed from time to time—although very rarely—by amendments to that constitution. This is the supreme law of the land. Secondly, the people, through their elected representatives in legislatures in all fifty states, and in Washington, D.C. on behalf of the federal (i.e., national) government, also pass laws. Laws passed by legislatures are frequently referred to as "statutes" in the everyday proceedings of the judicial system. Judges must apply the law found in the Constitution and in the statutes. Sometimes there will be inconsistencies between the Constitution and a statute. For example, the Constitution guarantees freedom of speech. Now imagine a statute that made it a crime to talk about communism on a street corner. Because the Constitution is the supreme law, a judge might decide that the statute is not constitutional, and in that case, the statute would be struck down by judicial order. It would no longer be in effect.

Sometimes a law is unclear, or sometimes a law itself says that it's up to the judge to decide what to do. Sometimes the law is found by reading past decisions of judges. In all these cases, judges have to decide what to do. They follow statutory language. When the language of the law itself is not clear, they try to follow the intent of the laws that do exist.

Judges exercise their discretion when authorized by law to do so. For example, it is left to the discretion of the trial judge to set bail, decide to exclude certain evidence from a trial even if it is technically relevant, and put limits on how much effort parties have to expend to deliver materials to the other side in pre-trial proceedings. (Most of these areas are discussed later in this book.)

In sum, it is judges who say what the law is. If judges apply statutory law, and the legislatures disagrees—if the elected representatives disagree with what a judge announced—then the legislature can change the law, or make it plainer. If a judge announces what she believes to be a requirement of the Constitution, and the people disagree, they can change the Constitution with another amendment. But as one famous Chief Justice of the U.S. Supreme Court said in 1803, "It is emphatically the province and duty of the judicial department [the courts] to say what the law is."

Juries and judges: facts and law

Judges and juries both make decisions at trial, but usually they have very different roles. Judges are responsible for knowing what the law is. Judges tell juries what the law is such as the definition of a charged crime. In a trial, judges rule on, say, which evidence can and cannot be presented to a jury. By contrast, the jury decides what the *facts* are: for example whether the light was red or green, whether someone was really under the influence of alcohol, whether someone broke a promise to pay money, and other factual issues. Juries have to decide whom to believe, when people testify as witnesses at trials. Based on their decisions about whom they believed and what really happened, the jury then decides the case. They decide if a defendant is guilty or not guilty in a criminal case, or whether the person bringing a civil case (the plaintiff) or the person who gets sued in a civil case (the defendant) should win. If the plaintiff wins, the jury decides how much money the plaintiff should receive.

People usually have a right to a jury trial, a right guaranteed by the Constitution. People do sometimes give up their right to a jury. They do this for a variety of reasons. First, trial by jury is slower than trial by a judge. It takes time to pick juries, and often proceedings have to be held first outside the jury's presence to determine whether or not the jury can hear the evidence, and if they can, then the evidence has to be taken again in front of the jury. Jury trials can be more expensive, as well. Second, some cases really don't depend on determining disputed facts; indeed, the two sides might agree on all the relevant facts, leaving only legal issues to be decided. Since a judge always decides the legal issues, such a case might as well be presented solely to a judge.

In some cases, there is no right to a jury at all, and the parties are compelled to present their case to a judge alone. These cases are relatively rare and usually involve a claim for something other than money. Most civil cases are suits for money, but sometimes the person bringing the case (the plaintiff) won't ask for money: he just wants a court order that something happen or not happen. For example, the plaintiff may seek an order than a neighbor remove a tree or fix a sewage outlet, or that a competitor company stop making false advertisements. In these cases, the parties probably will not have a right to a jury. The judge will make all the decisions.

If the trial is before the judge without a jury, then he does all the work the jury would do. This kind of a trial is called a *bench* trial, because we call the seat and desk where judges sit the 'bench'. Judges are sometimes referred to as bench officers, and when judges first become judges, or when they enter a courtroom, we say they *take the bench.*

The U.S. Constitution and the Supremacy Clause

As noted above, we have a written constitution, one that applies to the entire country; this is the U.S. Constitution. The fifty states each also have their own constitution, which within each state is the supreme law on matters of state law.

Federal law usually takes precedence, or trumps, state law. If there is an inconsistency between the U.S. Constitution and the constitution of, say, Delaware, the requirements of the U.S. Constitution must go into effect. This is because every state is bound by the U.S. Constitution first and foremost. In the U.S. Constitution, there is a provision known as the Supremacy Clause. The Supremacy Clause says:

> This constitution, and the Laws of the United States which shall be made in Pursuance thereof; and all Treaties made, or which shall be made, under the Authority of the United States, shall be the supreme Law of the Land; and the Judges in every State shall be bound thereby; any Thing in the Constitution or Laws of any State to the Contrary notwithstanding.

Every judge in the nation is bound by federal, or national law, and by the U.S. Constitution. If a law or constitution of any of the states is in conflict, then it must be disregarded and federal law must be followed.

14

Chapter 3: The State and the Federal Governments

There are state governments and one national, or federal, government. Each state has a governor who runs the executive branch, legislators who pass laws, and judges who determine what the law is, and apply the law.

The federal government is headed by the President of the United States who lives and works in Washington, D.C. The federal legislature, also known as Congress, is divided into two houses, the Senate and the House of Representatives. It also meets in Washington. The top federal judges sit on the U.S. Supreme Court in Washington D.C., but the rest of the federal judges who interpret and apply federal law sit in various cities all across the country so that all citizens can have easy geographic access to the federal justice system. The state and federal governments have different sets of responsibilities, different sets of laws, and so different kinds of cases come into state and federal courts.

Federal Responsibilities

The U.S. Constitution sets out the responsibilities of the national government. Generally speaking these are tasks that are best handled one way throughout the entire country, and involve situations in which coordination within the entire United States is useful. For example, the national government handles trade with other nations, making war, and maintaining the currency. Federal laws regulate trade and commerce between the states, and generally speaking crimes that take place across state lines are subject to federal jurisdiction. This includes crimes that are committed with the use of interstate facilities such as telecommunications and the internet. Crimes committed on federal property, such as in federal courthouses or national parks, are also, for that reason, federal crimes.

State Responsibilities

The U.S. Constitution holds that powers not allocated to the federal government are reserved to the states. That means that, unless the U.S. Constitution says the federal government has authority in a certain area (such as interstate commerce), then the issue, whatever it is, is to be handled by the states. Thus, most disputes over contracts, most crimes (murder, robbery, assault, driving while under the influence, and so on and so forth), property disputes and other cases are matters for the various states to regulate as they see fit. Disputes in those areas are handled by the state courts.

Chapter 4: The Three Branches

Governmental functions are divided among three branches of government. This is true at the federal level, and the states have the same three part structure. These three branches act as checks and balances to each other.

Legislative

State and federal legislatures make the laws. They decide, for example, which acts will be treated as crimes, and what the range of penalties or sentences will be. Laws regulate the full range of powers exercised by government: they regulate what our taxes are, how much governmental employees are paid, and whether certain acts will be the subject of a civil suit. Legislatures decide that the tax revenues collected will be spent in certain ways, whether that be highway repair, setting up a new police unit, funding hospitals—there is an almost infinite number of projects that legislatures can decide to fund.

Executive

The executive branch in each state is headed by a state governor, and in the federal government, by the President of the United States. The executive branch carries out the laws, or puts them into effect. The President carries out our foreign policy and is commander in chief of the armed forces. The federal executive branch is operated generally through a number of cabinet officers, such as the Secretary of State (overseeing foreign policy), Secretary of Defense (operating the armed services), Secretaries of Agriculture, Transportation, Heath and Human Services, Housing and Urban Development, the Attorney General (heading the justice department which enforces the laws) and others. States often have similar sorts of officers who handle matters at the state level.

The executive branch includes law enforcement agencies such as the police, highway patrol, and all forms of investigators who work for the state and federal governments. At the state level, this branch includes district attorneys (one for each county in the state), and the state attorney general, who are responsible for enforcement the law of the state. On the federal level, the executive branch includes the U.S. Attorney General, and the U.S. Attorneys (one for each of the federal districts in the nation), who are charged with enforcing federal law. Of course, federal law enforcement investigators such as the FBI, U.S. Customs, Secret Service, and so on, are also part of the executive branch.

Judicial

The federal judicial power is held by the federal judges who are, pursuant to the U.S. Constitution, appointed for life (although they can be removed by Congress if they are impeached). Each state also has judges who are elected or appointed in a variety of ways, and who serve for varying terms of office.

Although the states sometimes have different names for the various sorts of judges, their judicial branches all have a similar structure, which is also similar to the structure of the federal judiciary. In each case, at the lowest level, we have trial judges. These are the judges who preside at trials, where witnesses testify and juries serve. Above the trial judges we have judges who sit on the courts of appeals, i.e., appellate courts, who review the judgments and other decisions of the trial judges. Above those courts of appeals, we have a supreme court in each state, and one for the federal government.

The supreme courts don't have to take every case presented to them; they decide which cases really need to be heard. How do supreme courts do that? They don't try to fix problems unique to a single case—

that's the business of the intermediate appellate court. Rather, supreme courts try to figure out which cases are of more general interest. That is, they try to address instances in which an area of law is ambiguous in a way that matters to a lot of people, including situations where the intermediate courts of appeal are in conflict and some more general resolution is needed. Those are the sorts of cases that supreme courts take.

When a state supreme court decides an issue of *state* law, that supreme court is the final word. There's nowhere else to go with that case. But sometimes the state supreme court decides a matter of *federal* law— perhaps, for example, how far to extend the U.S. Constitution's guarantee of freedom of the press, or whether the U.S. Constitution's guarantees against unreasonable search and seizure (see the Fourth Amendment) bar a certain kind of search of someone's home. In those cases, which involve interpretation of *federal* law, anyone who loses at the level of the state supreme court can try to get the federal U.S. Supreme Court in Washington, D.C. to take the case. But again, the U.S. Supreme Court decides which cases it wants to hear.

Chapter 5: How the Judicial system is organized

Federal system

The nation is divided into federal circuits. The First Circuit encompasses some of the New England states; the Second Circuit includes New York, Connecticut and Rhode Island; the Third Circuit includes Pennsylvania, New Jersey, and Delaware; and so on. The Ninth Circuit is in the West, and includes California, Alaska, Hawaii, Oregon, Nevada, and some neighboring states. There is also a circuit court in Washington, D.C. We also have one circuit known as the Federal Circuit, which handles very specialized federal cases involving intellectual property such as patents, and claims made against the United States. All told, twelve of these appellate circuit courts serve the regions of the nation.

Within each Circuit, we have one or more districts, and we have federal district court judges in each of those districts. For example, the Ninth Circuit includes California and other western states. California is divided into the Northern District (with district trial courts in San Francisco and in San Jose), the Southern District (with district trial court in San Diego), and the Eastern District (with district trial courts in Sacramento and Fresno). Because of its relatively low population, Nevada is just one district, although the federal district court judges sit in a few different cities. Rhode Island, New Hampshire, and many other states too have only one district. New York has four. Many individual district court judges serve in each district.

Judgments of those trial judges are appealed to the regional Circuit Courts of Appeals, and those Courts of Appeals are in turn responsible to the U.S. Supreme Court in Washington, D.C.

Judges on the federal district court, on the Courts of Appeals, and on the Supreme Court are appointed by the President of the United States and confirmed by the U.S. Senate. They cannot be removed from office, unless they are impeached and removed by Congress. For this reason, federal judges are said to have life tenure. This makes them independent, and protects them from political influence or any temptation to play to the crowd.

Bankruptcy judges

There are certain kinds of cases in the federal system which are heard by a special type of judge. These are bankruptcy cases. People and companies who find themselves over their heads in debt can declare bankruptcy under federal law. Also, creditors—those to whom money is owed—can force a debtor into bankruptcy. The bankruptcy court will take over all the assets of the person or company, such as property, income, and so on, and come up with a plan to pay off the creditors, at least to some extent. Sometimes, it's necessary to decide whether or not the bankrupt person (the debtor) really owes the money. For example, it may be necessary to decide whether or not the bankrupt owes money under a contract. These cases can be tried in front of the bankruptcy judge.

U.S. magistrate judges

Magistrate judges are actually hired by the federal district court judges (the trial judges) in a district. They are not appointed by the President or confirmed by the Senate, and they do not have life tenure. They usually have terms of eight years, which are renewed by their bosses--the district court which hired them--if they are doing a satisfactory job. Magistrate judges help take the load off the shoulders of the district court judges by handling settlement conferences and discovery disputes. Discovery disputes and settlement conferences will be discussed later, but for now it is enough to note that in civil cases parties exchange demands for information, which often leads to disputes on how much information one side needs to provide to the other. Rulings of magistrate judges on discovery disputes, or anything else, can generally be appealed to a district court judge.

Parties also may agree that their case can be heard by a magistrate judge, just as if he or she were a district court judge. If the parties agree, the magistrate judge will decide all the issues in the case, and will conduct the trial. When that happens, the rulings of the magistrate judge are appealed directly to the regional Court of Appeals, in the very same way as a ruling by district court judges.

Federal district (trial) courts

Trials in the federal judicial system are conducted by district court judges. There are 94 districts in the United States and its possessions, and each has a varying number of judges assigned. When people wish to file a lawsuit (a "civil" case), or when the federal prosecutor wishes to charge someone with a crime (a "criminal" case), those cases are filed in the district court. After pretrial preparation, efforts to settle the case, and other procedures, they go to trial. At trial there is a verdict—one side wins and the other loses. With one exception, the party who loses can appeal to the Court of Appeals. The exception is in a criminal trial when the jury (or the judge) has a verdict of not guilty. Those "not guilty" verdicts usually cannot be appealed and the defendant cannot be tried again.

Of course only *federal* criminal and civil cases can be filed in district courts. The U.S. Congress defines federal crimes in statutes. Federal crimes include offenses such as interstate transportation of stolen goods, mail fraud (the U.S. Government controls the U.S. mails), theft of federal government property including checks issued by the federal government, threats against the President of the United States, hijacking aircraft, use of the means of interstate commerce (such as telephone wires or the internet) to defraud anyone; evading federal taxes, and so on.

Some crimes can be handled by either the state or federal governments, such as bank robbery: banks are federally insured, so federal prosecutors can take the case. But it's also against state law to rob a bank, and thus state prosecutors also can take the case. Federal and state law enforcement authorities will agree on which of the two jurisdictions should take the case. Practically speaking, the more serious crimes, or those which overlap many states, are handled by the federal authorities.

In the same way, only certain types of civil cases can be filed in federal district court. There has to be *federal jurisdiction* to allow a federal judge to handle a case. If the judge is not convinced she has federal jurisdiction, she will dismiss the case. If that happens, the person bringing the lawsuit usually can file the case in state court.

There are two kinds of federal jurisdiction. The first is called *federal question* jurisdiction: that is, when the case presents an issue of federal law. For example, Congress passed an antitrust statute which makes it illegal for competitors to fix prices, to agree on what they will sell their products for. A federal prosecutor can file a criminal case against the conspirators for price fixing. But another company, or a consumer, which is injured by the price fixing conspiracy can file a federal *civil* suit and recover money. That civil suit depends on a federal question—that is, the application of federal antitrust law. So that case is filed in federal court. Since the U.S. Congress has passed laws about intellectual property, such as patents, trademarks, and copyright, those cases likewise involve federal questions and are brought in federal court. There are many other sorts of cases in which Congress has passed a law allowing certain types of civil suits: these all present federal questions and so are filed in federal district court.

There is a second kind of federal jurisdiction- which is known as *diversity* jurisdiction. Here, it doesn't matter what the questions or issues are in the case. What matters is *which states the parties are from*. If they are from different states—if they are *diverse* in that way—then the federal court will take the case. So for example if there is a car accident in San

Francisco between a citizen of California and a citizen from Nevada, and they sue each other, the case could be filed in California state courts— there's no federal question. But the case could *instead* be filed in federal district court in San Francisco (the Northern District of California) because the parties are from different states. The reason for diversity jurisdiction is to ensure that no one is discriminated against by the local courts. The Nevada citizen might feel that she would be at a disadvantage with a California state judge handling a case where the other side was a local California resident. Thus, cases which involve purely questions of local, or state law, can be found in federal courts if the parties are from different states.

Circuit Courts of Appeals

The regional Circuit Courts of Appeals hear appeals from the district courts in their circuits. Thus the Ninth Circuit Court of Appeals hears all the appeals from federal district courts in Oregon, California, Washington, and Hawaii; the Fourth Circuit Court of Appeals hears appeals from federal trial courts in Virginia, and so on. Some special kinds of cases, such as intellectual property patent cases, are heard by the Federal Circuit Court of Appeals, no matter where the trial was held. There is a D.C. Circuit Court of Appeals as well, in Washington, D.C., which takes cases solely from district courts in the nation's capital. While it might appear that such an appellate court would have very little work to do, it turns out that many federal cases are tried in Washington, D.C., which is, after all, where virtually all federal agencies are located. So D.C. is its own Circuit, and has its own Circuit Court of Appeals.

There are many judges assigned to each Circuit Court of Appeals. But these courts assign only three of the judges to each case; we say they sit in three judge panels. This helps manage the heavy workload. Sometimes the three judges disagree, and if so, then the case is decided by the majority of the three judges.

Sometimes a case is so important that that the Court believes that all the judges should hear the case, and then they will have a new argument in front of all the judges; this known as hearing a case *en banc.* This is in effect a second hearing in the appellate court. In the Ninth Circuit, there are actually too many judges to do this, so they arrange *"en banc"* courts of eleven judges each for these sorts of important cases. There is another reason for convening an *en banc* court: a panel of three judges must follow the precedent of its court, whether it wants to or not. Sometimes it's wise to reconsider precedent, and take a fresh view of a legal issue. Three judge panels are not free to do that, but the court *en banc* can do that and can overrule precedent.

Every Circuit has a Chief Judge who runs the administration of the court. But the Chief Judge doesn't have any more of a vote than any other judge when it comes to deciding cases.

U.S. Supreme Court

The United States Supreme Court is in Washington, D.C., across the street from the U.S. Capitol Building. The judges of the Court are known as Justices; one refers, for example, to Justice Scalia or Justice Souter. The head of the Court is the Chief Justice, but he is not only the head of that Court, he is also the head of the entire federal judicial system, and so his title is in fact Chief Justice of the United States, *not* the Chief Justice of the Supreme Court. In addition to the Chief, eight other justices—Associate Justices—sit on the Court. Each of the nine justices has the same vote when it comes to deciding cases. All nine justices vote on how to decide each case.

Unlike the various Circuit Courts of Appeal, the Supreme Court chooses which cases to take. Parties who have lost their appeal in the federal Circuit Courts of Appeal, and those who have lost their cases in the various state Supreme Courts, can ask the U.S. Supreme Court to take their cases. To do this, they file a paper called a petition for a *writ of certiorari.*

It takes four of the nine Justices to agree to take a case, to "grant cert." In fact, almost all "cert petitions" are denied. When the Supreme Court has denied a cert petition, it means that the ruling below—the ruling in the Circuit Court of Appeals or the state supreme court—stands as the law of that case. But it does *not* mean that the U.S. Supreme Court actually agrees with what happened below; it means only that the U.S. Supreme Court doesn't think the case is important enough to hear. Very often the news and media will report that the U.S. Supreme Court has "affirmed" or "agreed" with the lower court decision when all it did was to deny cert. These news reports are wrong. Denying cert simply means that the Supreme Court could not muster four votes to take the case.

After the Court accepts and determines a case, it may do many things. It might affirm or reverse the judgment of the Court of Appeals (or state supreme court). It might vacate the ruling below and send it back for further consideration.

There is another situation in which the Supreme Court takes a case, but does not decide it. Suppose one Justice is sick, or for some other reason does not participate in the case (maybe there's a conflict of interest, such as when a Justice owns stock in a company which has a case in the Court), and the remainder of the Justices split 4-4 on how to decide a matter. Then there is no majority opinion for the court, and the lower court ruling is in effect affirmed. But again, this does *not* mean the Supreme Court agrees with the lower court's opinion.

If the case is from a state supreme court, the U.S. Supreme Court won't hear it if it involves solely issues of state law, because the *state* Supreme courts are the final word on what *state* law is. Of course there is an exception: imagine a diversity case which involves only state law issues, and the case is appealed to the regional Circuit Court of Appeals. Technically, the U.S. Supreme Court might take the case; but probably it won't.

If cert is granted in a case, then the U.S. Supreme Court Justices read the briefs and hear oral argument. The Court then affirms or reverses the decision below. Sometimes the Court realizes that cert never should have been granted, and it in effect just dismisses the case and sends it back to the intermediate appellate court below.

There are some very special cases which actually are filed for the first time directly in the U.S. Supreme Court. These cases never have been heard in e.g. a federal trial or appellate court. For example, suits between states are filed directly with the U.S. Supreme Court, and the Court has to have a form of trial. One state might sue another over, for example, rights to water in a river they share, or to determine a border between states. The Supreme Court does not in fact have trials in its courtroom, only oral arguments. Therefore, if the Court needs to have facts presented, testimony heard, exhibits reviewed, or other evidence accumulated, the Court needs a procedure by which these materials can be brought before the Justices. This is done by appointing a respected lawyer or judge, called a Special Master. The Special Master conducts the hearings perhaps in an office or other location, and it is the Special Master who will actually have the hearing, take testimony, review the documents, and make a recommendation for the final result. The U.S. Supreme Court then has oral argument based on all the work by the Special Master and decides the case.

State System

A good example of a state court system is that of California. It is in fact the largest judicial system in the world—with more judges than any other state or nation including the U.S. federal judicial system. California has a state supreme court which hears cases in its main San Francisco location, as well as in Sacramento and Los Angeles. Below the supreme court we have the state courts of appeal, and below those the superior courts, where trials are held. The trial courts in California are called "superior" courts because many years ago California also had *municipal* courts which handled the smaller cases, and appeals from the municipal court went to the superior courts. Now, all the work of the superior and municipal courts is consolidated in the superior courts.

To provide a sense of how cases filter up through the court system, consider these numbers from the fiscal year 2004-2005:

In all the Superior Courts, about nine million cases were filed.

In the state courts of appeal, about twenty-four thousand appeals were filed—about .003 percent of the cases handled in the superior courts. (This number appears relatively low, because the massive superior court total includes all cases, even small claims, traffic and other matters, which are virtually never appealed).

In the same period, the Supreme Court had about nine thousand matters filed with it, 5410 of which were petitions seeking the reversal of a court of appeals ruling. The state Supreme Court issued 125 opinions actually deciding a case—that is, in about 0.023% of the petitions filed for review of an appellate decision. Only the tiniest fraction of cases in which a party wants the Supreme Court to rule does that Court actually issue an opinion.

In California, Superior court (trial) and appellate judges (Courts of Appeal and Supreme Court—these judges are known as "justices") get their jobs in different ways. Superior court judges are elected by the citizens in their county for six year terms. If there is a vacancy—say, because a judge resigns, retires, is removed, or is appointed to higher office—then the Governor appoints a judge to fill out the remainder of the six year term. As a matter of fact, most judges take office in this way. The judges then go on to stand for election for the next six year term. If no one opposes the judge, he or she wins the election automatically. But someone can run against the judge in that election, and if he or she wins, the incumbent judge loses the position and the newcomer becomes a judge.

The appellate justices (including those on the state Supreme Court) are always appointed by the Governor, and must be approved by a three person committee made up of the Attorney General, the Presiding Justice of the Court to which the judge is to be appointed, and the Chief Justice of the

State of California. Appellate justices have 12 year terms, and too are appointed to fill out the terms of the justice they are replacing. When that term is up, no one can run against the appellate justice in an election, but the people of the state can vote to retain, or not retain, the justice. If the vote is not to retain, then the justice loses the appellate position and the Governor must make another appointment.

State Supreme Court

The California Supreme Court has seven justices. On all matters of interpreting and applying state law, this Supreme Court is all powerful and its opinions are binding on all lower California courts. The Supreme Court is led by the Chief Justice of the State. State courts often have to decide issues of federal law—after all, federal law is supreme and binds every judge in the nation—and so issues of federal law may arise in cases before the California Supreme Court. On those federal issues, the California Supreme Court, like every other court in the land, must follow the law as set forth by the U.S. Supreme Court. Like the U.S. Supreme Court, most cases are heard by the California Supreme Court only after a petition is filed in that court and the court agrees to take the case. As with the U.S. Supreme Court, most cases are turned away, and the Court expresses no opinion. A major exception to this is any death penalty case. In every case in which the death penalty is imposed, the California Supreme Court must hear the appeal.

Courts of Appeal

The California courts of appeal are called the First Appellate District Court of Appeal, the Second Appellate District Court of Appeal, and so on. The state is divided into six such "Districts" and all the final judgments of the trial courts—the superior courts—in each such District may be appealed to the governing District Court of Appeal. (Be careful! Do *not* confuse this use of the word 'district' with the way that word is used to describe the *federal* trial courts, which are known as 'district' courts.) As with their federal counterparts, judges on these appellate courts sit in panels of three judges each. Parties who lose their case in the trial court (the Superior Court) have a right to appeal their final judgments to the court of appeal; the courts of appeal *must* hear those cases.

The courts of appeal can also decide *writ petitions*. These petitions are filed by parties when they are dissatisfied with a ruling of a trial court, but the ruling is not the final judgment. There is an infinite sea of decisions of trial courts which are subject to these sorts of writ proceedings—decisions about how to pick a jury, what questions are asked at trial, what sort of materials one party has to produce to the other side in pre-trial proceedings, and so on. The courts of appeal do not have to hear these writs—it's purely optional. Writs are issued only when it's a real emergency, the issues can't be corrected later on a regular appeal after a final judgment, and the consequences of an erroneous lower trial court ruling are very serious. Probably less than one per cent of writ petitions are granted.

Superior Courts

Trials are held in the superior courts. This is where most citizens will interact with the justice system.

There is a superior court in each of California's 58 counties, but there is a wide difference in the number of judges assigned to each such court, depending on the population of that county. For example, there are two judges in Alpine County, and hundreds of judges in Los Angeles county. In San Francisco County, where one of the authors sits as a judge, there are about 50 judges. The superior courts also employ court commissioners, which, like their counterparts in the federal system, magistrate judges, are hired by the judges to assist in a wide variety of areas. Sometimes the parties will agree that a court commissioner can act as a superior court judge, in which case the commissioner has all the authority of a superior court judge.

As is true of their federal counterparts, superior court judges preside at trial, which means they govern the proceedings. They rule on evidentiary objections; that is, they decide if evidence (testimony, or some document) can be heard or shown to the jury. They sentence defendants who are convicted of crimes. They review and authorize search and arrest warrants. Generally, they ensure a fair and orderly process in the court, in compliance with the law.

As the introductory short story in this book suggested, most cases fit into one of two types: (a) criminal proceedings where the state brings charges where the penalty can be either (or both) a fine or jail or prison time, and (b) civil cases, where one party, the plaintiff, sues another party, the defendant, usually to get money damages. One case also can involve many plaintiffs and many defendants.

Superior courts also have other types of cases. For example, traffic tickets are handled by commissioners. In addition, there is a "small claims" type of case in which if the plaintiff is seeking $7,500 or less, the plaintiff can file a small claims form and have the case heard on an expedited basis, before a judge (no jury)—in fact, often before a commissioner who sits as judge with the approval of the parties. If the plaintiff loses, he cannot appeal. But if the defendant loses—the defendant who may *not* have chosen or wished to have the case heard in small claims—the defendant can appeal to another judge on the Superior Court. Because people don't have lawyers in small claims trials, because there are no juries, and because the cases are heard in much less time than the usual civil case, it is far less expensive to use the small claims system.

Superior courts also have probate departments, which handle wills, and juvenile and family departments. The juvenile departments handle cases involving youths under 18, and the family court takes care of disputes between parents, such as divorces and child support issues.

Chapter 6: Criminal Law vs. Civil Law

Most cases filed in court are either civil cases or criminal cases. Civil cases involve disputes among people or companies. Criminal cases are filed when the government alleges that a person (or, sometimes, a company) has committed an illegal act. As we have seen from the introductory scenario, often the same events—for example, a car accident—can lead to both a civil and criminal proceeding. The party that brings, or starts, the case is usually called the *plaintiff*; the person or company defending is generally called the *defendant*.

Civil and criminal cases have many procedures in common and there are also very important differences between the two types of cases. For example, in a civil case, a jury can issue its decision (a verdict) without every single person on the jury agreeing to it. In California state court, nine of 12 jurors are enough for a verdict. But in a criminal case, all twelve jurors must agree. In a civil case, a juror votes for whichever side has proved its case by a "preponderance of the evidence," that is, the side which has the stronger argument, even if it's only slightly stronger. One might imagine a balance scale, with the evidence from both sides on scales, and the scales tipping ever so slightly to one side: that side would win the civil case. But in a *criminal* case the plaintiff—which is called the "People" in state court and the "Government" in the federal court—must prove its case "beyond a reasonable doubt," which is a much higher standard of proof.

The next sections will briefly discuss some aspects of these two types of cases.

Criminal Cases

The government through its legislative branch passes laws which define what a crime is. These statutes also set the limits on what the sentence, or penalty, can be for someone who is found guilty of committing a crime. Here's an example from California:

> *Penal Code § 5890*
>
> Every person who maliciously removes, destroys, injures, breaks or defaces any mile post, board, or stone, or guide-post erected on or near any highway, or any inscription thereon, is guilty of a misdemeanor.

What is a *misdemeanor*? Generally misdemeanors are crimes which are punishable by imprisonment in the county jail for up to six months or a year and/or a fine of up to $1,000.00. There are crimes which have more serious consequences, which are called felonies. A felony is punishable by more than a year in state prison. For example, in California state courts, a felony (e.g., selling illegal drugs) might be punishable by a term in state prison of 16 months, or 2 or 3 years. The judge decides, at the time of sentencing, which of those three terms is to be imposed for that felony.

Most of the crimes in California are described in the Penal Code, but there are many other codes as well which define crimes. For example, driving under the influence of alcohol or drugs is described in the Vehicle Code:

> *Vehicle Code § 23152 Driving While Under the Influence of Alcohol or Drugs*
>
> (a)   It is unlawful for any person who is under the influence of any alcoholic beverage or drug, or under the

combined influence of any alcoholic beverage and drug, to drive a vehicle.

(b)   It is unlawful for any person who has 0.08 percent or more, by weight, of alcohol in his or her blood to drive a vehicle.

There are two crimes set out here, one under (a) and one under (b). A person might be charged and convicted of either, or of both, these crimes. The sentences for these two crimes are set forth in other sections of the Vehicle Code.

The state legislature also passes laws which provide for many of the procedures used in criminal cases, such as what sort of evidence the prosecution has to give to the defendant, and vice versa. Certain kinds of pre-trial hearings, too, are described and required by statutes.

Constitutional Rights

Defendants in criminal cases enjoy certain constitutional rights. These rights are described in both state constitutions and the U.S. Constitution which, because of the Supremacy Clause, is also binding on every state. Federal courts are bound only by the U.S. Constitution. Generally, the protections offered by the state and federal constitutions are almost exactly the same. Some of the most important constitutional guarantees are found the U.S. Constitution in the Fourth, Fifth, and Sixth Amendments. We discuss these important rights next.

The Fourth Amendment (protection from unreasonable search & seizure)

The Fourth Amendment bars unreasonable searches and seizures. The issue comes up in many criminal cases, such as for example when the police arrest someone, or when they search a car or home and find illegal items such as drugs or unregistered guns, or evidence such as blood stains, documents, money, and so on.

Under the Fourth Amendment of the U.S. Constitution, searches by the police have to be *reasonable*. That means one of two things. Either the police had a search warrant, or they otherwise acted reasonably in conducting a search without a warrant.

Search warrants are issued by judges. The police or other law enforcement authorities prepare a sworn statement which outlines why they think they have "probable cause" to think that items associated with a crime will be found in a specific location. Those things can be drugs, weapons, or other evidence. For example, the police might have witnesses who saw a drug deal on the street, and then saw the dealer enter a house. The judge on those facts might authorize a search of the house for drugs, money, lists of clients, and other materials which might reasonably be found there that relate to the crime of drug dealing. The police may search only in the specific places stated in the search warrant, i.e., the bedroom, the closets, the kitchen, etc. A search warrant that authorizes a search of someone's apartment exclusively does not authorize a search of that person's car.

Sometimes the police do not have time to get a warrant. For example, a highway patrol officer might see a driver weaving all over the highway, apparently drunk. The officer may stop the car and perform a search such as taking a blood sample, or seizing an open bottle of beer, without a warrant. Or if the police are chasing a person who has just shot someone else and flees into a home, then police can chase and search the home for him. Under those circumstances, the police usually do not have to wait to get a warrant from a judge.

After the arrest, the defendant can challenge the search warrant if there was in fact not enough of a showing made to the judge who issued it. When judges issue search warrants, they review statements made under oath by the police and others assisting the police. Those sworn statements must show that there is a fair probability that the items sought by the police will be found in the described location. If the sworn statements actually don't provide any basis for making this determination by the judge, or if the statements were in fact false—perjury—then a judge may decide that the warrant never should have been issued, and as a consequences items seized under the authority of the search warrant cannot be used at trial against the defendant. This is called *exclusion* of the evidence, and the rule (developed by the U.S. Supreme Court) barring the use of this wrongfully seized evidence is called the *exclusionary rule*. The theory is that the police, the District Attorney, and the prosecuting team generally will be encouraged to act appropriately if they know that bad behavior will give them no advantage in terms of collecting evidence.

The defendant also can challenge the search done without a warrant, for example by arguing that the police did not have a reasonable basis for thinking the defendant had fled, or had done anything such as weaving around the highway.

In these challenges, the defendant asks the judge to find that the searches were unreasonable and if they are, then the evidence cannot be used at trial against the defendant—the evidence is "suppressed" under the exclusionary rule. These hearings are called suppression hearings. If the evidence is suppressed by the judge, often that results in dismissal of the charges, because there is no evidence the government can use at trial.

The Fifth Amendment ("right not to incriminate oneself," also known as "*Miranda* rights")

Defendants have rights guaranteed by the Fifth Amendment not to be compelled to give evidence against themselves. The government cannot force a confession. In a series of cases including the famous *Miranda* decision, the U.S. Supreme Court ruled that, to give real effect to this important constitutional right, the police (or other law enforcement authorities) have to tell the defendant, after he has been arrested, that he in fact *has* this right. The Court also has ruled that coercion is considered to take place not only in the obvious ways, such as torture and beatings, but also if people feel coerced once they are in custody, surrounded by police, and being asked questions about an offenses. Therefore the Court ruled that the so-called *Miranda* warnings have to be given to a defendant once he has been arrested, before he can be asked to confess or otherwise be asked to talk about the crime. If a statement or confession is taken without the police having taken these steps, then the confession is suppressed and cannot be used to convict the defendant.

The Sixth Amendment ("right to a lawyer" or *Gideon*)

Defendants also have the right to be represented by a lawyer. If they cannot afford a lawyer, the government must provide one free of charge. This is why we have Public Defenders Offices: they are lawyers who specialize in criminal defense work and are paid by the government. The right to have a lawyer, at state expense if necessary, harkens back to the famous *Gideon* case decided by the U.S. Supreme Court in 1963. Before then, if a defendant could not afford a lawyer he had to make do without.

The Sixth Amendment ("right to a jury")

The Sixth Amendment of the U.S. Constitution, and many similar state constitutional provisions, guarantee a defendant a right to a jury trial. This right does not extend to infractions, where the maximum penalty does not include any jail time. It does extend to most misdemeanors and the more serious crimes known as felonies. The Sixth Amendment does more than simply guarantee a jury, however: the jury trial must be "speedy and public." If the authorities wait too long, the case may be dismissed as a result of that violation of the constitutional right. We provide a copy of an order dismissing a case for just this reason in the appendices of this book.

Waiving or giving up rights

All rights can be waived, or given up. For example, we have a right to a jury trial. But a defendant can decide to plead guilty, in which case he is waiving his right to a jury trial. A defendant can waive his right to a lawyer. He can waive his right to a speedy trial. All rights can be waived, as long as it is clear that the defendant understands what it is that he is waiving. That is, a waiver must be *knowing*.

People waive their Fourth Amendment rights, for example, when a police officer asks if he can look inside a bag, or asks if he may inspect the trunk of a car and inside a home, and the person agrees. People waive their Fifth Amendment rights when the police tell them they have the right to remain silent, and then ask the defendant if he'd like to talk to them; if he says yes, he's waived his right to remain silent. People can waive their right to a lawyer. In fact, the courts have held that people have a right to represent themselves, so that if a person refuses to be represented by a lawyer, and the court finds he is basically competent and understands his rights and the disadvantages of representing himself, he can waive his right to a lawyer and represent himself throughout the criminal proceedings.

Civil Cases

There is a wide range of civil cases. Often, people and companies sue each other for breach of contract. For example, if someone promises to buy a house for a hundred thousand dollars and then refuses to pay the money, the other side would sue for what are termed *money damages*, that is, the money he is owed under the contract to sell the house. Any breach of an agreement can result in a civil suit. Employers and employees can sue each other over employment contracts. Civil suits include disputes between neighbors—for example, disputes over boundaries, whether a fence or tree encroaches on the other's land. Generally, any case where the executive branch is *not* involved is a civil case.

Torts are also the subject of civil suits. A tort is any injury to another, or to another's property, by reason of e.g., negligence. So if one driver crashes into another and the second car is damaged or the second driver is hurt, the second driver can sue the first driver for money damages, alleging the tort of negligence. Under this theory, people can sue for tripping or slipping on someone else's property, doctors and lawyers can be sued for their negligence, manufacturers of asbestos can be sued when others inhale their asbestos fibers and get sick; and so on.

States and the federal government also create specific types of rights or expectations. Breaching such a right can be the basis for a lawsuit. For example, statutes define what a "trade secret" is—that is, some piece of secret knowledge that gives the owner of a company a commercial advantage over his competition. A trade secret might be the formula for Coca Cola, computer code, or a special way to make furniture in half the time it takes someone else. If someone takes that trade secret without approval, he can be sued.

There are other types of "property" created by laws called "intellectual property". These sorts of "properties" includes (1) trademarks (e.g. the logo used by various companies under which they sell their products, like *Nike* for shoes, or the distinctive large yellow "M" used by the McDonald's fast food chain, or *iPod* for Apple's MP3 music player), (2) copyrights (the ownership a person has in things he creates such as sculptures, poems, novels, music, and so on) and (3) patents (inventions). If someone without authority takes or uses that intellectual property, he can be sued by the owner.

In addition, there are privacy rights. Privacy rights and expectations can be the subject of federal, or state, law, and if a person invades someone else's privacy, he can be sued. For example, if someone takes medical or financial information without permission, he may be sued.

There are many other sorts of civil cases as well.

In civil cases, there are usually two kinds of relief the plaintiff is seeking against the defendant. The first is money damages; the second is injunctive relief.

Usually the plaintiff wants money to compensate her for her injuries, or for other damage the defendant has done to her. If the acts of the defendant were truly outrageous, the plaintiff may seek punitive damages, which are also money damages but are not designed to compensate the plaintiff for the injuries she suffered. Rather, the jury awards a sum of money to punish the defendant. For example, punitive damages might be awarded against a car manufacturer which delivered an unsafe car; or against a company that was outrageously negligent in the creation of a massive oil spill. Punitive damages have been sought against tobacco companies under the theory that they knew at the time of sale that cigarettes led to cancer but never told the consuming public.

In a jury trial, it is the jury that decides how much money to award. Juries decide how much to award for compensatory damages, as well as how much to award for punitive damages. Of course, the jury first has to decide the case in favor of the plaintiff and against the defendant.

As noted, plaintiffs usually ask for *money* damages. The second kind of relief sought by plaintiffs is *injunctive relief.* Injunctions are issued by courts: that is, judges, not juries. Injunctions direct someone to do something, or not to do something. An injunction might stop one company from buying another, or it might stop someone from cutting a tree down, or might require someone to cut down a tree. Injunctions are issued to stop people from falsely passing off their products as an imitation of someone else's products. An injunction might require a company to shut down a web site, or might require the government to continue making welfare payments, or stop a death penalty from being carried out, or might put a limit on the number of prisoners a state can have in a single building. Almost anything can be the subject of an injunction.

People ask for injunctions at different times in the life of a civil case. If there is an emergency at the very beginning of a case, a plaintiff can ask for a *temporary restraining order*, also known as a TRO. You might need a TRO if your neighbor was about to cut down a tree which you believe actually sits on your own land—you can't afford to wait for, say, two years for the lawsuit about who owns the tree to be over if the defendant is going to cut the tree down tomorrow morning. TROs are issued only in real emergencies, and they always expire very quickly, usually in about 10 days, because often the judge only has information from one side (from the plaintiff), and not the other, and has no good idea what the defendant's position is.

Plaintiff can also then seek a *preliminary injunction* which is an injunction that is issued before the verdict, and is in place for the duration of the case, but not longer. So, for example, in the tree case, after the TRO expires, the plaintiff will probably ask for a preliminary injunction. The judge will set a time for a hearing, and will get evidence from both sides— although not as much as the judge would get at trial. But at least both sides have a chance to prepare, and to present their case to the judge. The judge will balance the chances of ultimate success, the harm to each side if the injunction is granted or not granted, the extent to which money damages can take care of any injury if the injunction is not granted, and then will issue (or not) the preliminary injunction. That injunction will expire at the end of the case, and so it might be in place for some years as the case is litigated in the trial court, goes up on appeal, and so on.

Finally, at the end of the case, any preliminary injunction expires. At that point, the court may (if the plaintiff wins the case!) issue a *permanent injunction*. As the name implies, this order is in place forever, or up to a date set by the court, unless the court terminates it for some reason later. For example, a judge might issue a permanent injunction that the Fire Department take steps to integrate the Department racially and by gender (i.e. hire more minorities and women). Perhaps fifteen or twenty years later, the Fire Department will feel it has done enough and will ask that the injunction be dissolved. The court might issue a permanent injunction, after trial, that bars one company from using the trademarks that belong to another company.

Court can both issue injunctions, and make money damages awards (as the result of a jury decision), in the same case.

Chapter 7: Introduction to the Hierarchy of Law

As suggested above under the discussions of the Supremacy Clause, there is a hierarchy to the structure of laws. Some laws trump, or supersede, others. The issue arises because laws are made in a variety of ways, and different laws sometimes try to govern the same subject matter. For example, a City Council might wish to pass a law banning all hand guns from the city. But there may be a state law that regulates hand guns, allowing them throughout the state as long as the owner registers the gun. The city and state laws conflict.

Or assume that the federal government passes a law allowing trucks to have axles eight feet long, but a state passes a law requiring all trucks to have axles not more than seven feet long. Because the same trucks are sold throughout the country, and trucks sold in one state may well pass through other states, the truck manufacturers will be subject to inconsistent state and federal law. In the case of conflicts, there must be a way to tell which law is supreme.

As you may anticipate, federal law usually (but not always!) supersedes state law, and state law usually supersedes local (e.g., city) law. And within each of the state and federal systems, there is a further hierarchy of laws: the federal U.S. Constitution supersedes other federal law, and state constitutions supersede state statutes. "Supersede" in this sense means that, if a judge is confronted with two inconsistent laws, say one from the federal government and one from the state government, and the federal government is authorized to have passed its law, then the state law is invalid and the judge will not follow it. The state law will have no effect.

In the chapters that follow, we will briefly describe the types of federal law, and then the types of state law, and then we will discuss the way in which judges may be said to "make" law.

Chapter 8: Federal Law

Federal law consists of the U.S. (federal) Constitution, treaties with other nations, and laws passed by Congress. Federal law applies throughout the United States, and so both federal and state judges are bound by it.

The Constitution

The U.S. Constitution (which includes its Amendments) is the most important document in the United States, and is the supreme law of the land. This document is the keystone of our system of government and the foundation of our judicial system. Every citizen should read it. Every public official, and every judge, swears to uphold the U.S. Constitution in the oath of office. The Constitution describes the responsibilities of each of the three branches of government, including judges whose jobs are set out in Article III, which is why federal judges are sometimes called "Article III judges." The Constitution sets out the responsibility of the federal government as a whole, and reserves other powers not enumerated to the States. The Constitution contains the bedrock freedoms which are so much a hallmark of the remarkable experiment in representative democracy we call the United States: freedom of religion and of speech, freedom from unreasonable searches and seizures, and equal protection under the law, among others.

Federal Treaties

The United States, as a government, makes agreements with other nations: these agreements are treaties. Treaties cover issues such as international trade, the making of war, global environmental issues, use and acquisition of lands and so on. Because it is essential that the United States speak with one voice in these contexts, treaties supersede all other U.S. laws, state and federal, except the U.S. Constitution.

Federal Statutes

Congress, by passing bills in the Senate and the House of Representatives, enacts statutes, that is, federal laws. Almost all of these are printed in the U.S. Code. For example, Title 18 of the U.S. Code contains most of the criminal statutes, and there are many volumes for that title. Congress may pass laws on any subject which are "necessary and proper" (to quote the U.S. Constitution) to its exercise of its constitutional powers. Those powers are listed in the U.S. Constitution at Article I section 8, and include, for example, the powers to borrow money, establish post offices, protect intellectual property, raise and support the armed forces, handle interstate commerce, and regulate money. The courts have been generally expansive in their view of what is "necessary and proper" and thus most laws which are reasonably related to the enumerated Congressional powers are constitutional.

Chapter 9: State Law

The hierarchy of state laws is very similar to the federal hierarchy. Above all state laws, of course, is federal law; but within the areas not given to federal power by the U.S. Constitution, the states' law reigns supreme. Within each state, its state constitution will be the supreme state law. The state legislatures pass laws which, if constitutional, must be followed, and local and municipal governments also may pass laws in areas reserved to them.

When State Law Supersedes Federal Law - the 10th Amendment

As discussed, federal law usually supersedes state law. Assume for example that Congress passes a law that all highway speed limits are at 60 miles per hour. The Wisconsin legislature passes a law that cars may drive up to 100 miles an hour within its borders, and the state law is challenged. A judge will first determine whether Congress was authorized to enact its 60 m.p.h. statute. Because it appears reasonably related to interstate commerce, one of the enumerated federal powers, the judge will probably find the federal law constitutional. And because the federal law conflicts with the Wisconsin law, the judge will strike down the Wisconsin law because the federal law is supreme.

But the Tenth Amendment to the U.S. Constitution expressly reserves to the states the powers not granted to the federal government. The federal government is one of limited powers. That means that federal courts, too, are courts of limited jurisdiction: they simply cannot take a case unless there is express authorization to do so. By contrast, we sometimes say that state courts are courts of general jurisdiction—state judges can handle any case filed in state court (except, of course, cases which are reserved solely to the federal courts).

Imagine a situation in which Congress passes a law that is outside its authority. For example, assume Congress passes a law requiring that fences around homes to be no higher than three feet. State and municipal laws (usually zoning laws) exist that regulate such things, and we may suppose such laws permit fences six feet high. A judge will look to the connection between federal powers as set forth in the U.S. Constitution, and determine whether there is some reasonable connection to the three foot high limit. What sort of *federal* interest is served by limiting fences to three feet? Doubtless, arguments can be made, perhaps involving the availability nationwide of fencing materials, but the arguments seem weak, and the judge is likely to declare the federal law unconstitutional, leaving the state law in place. Although the fence example is trivial, other very important issues along these lines do come up. For example, in the past Congress has passed laws regulating possession of firearms, and certain kinds of sexual assault, which have been challenged on the basis that there is no legitimate *federal* interest in these areas and any legislation must be left to the states.

Therefore, while federal law usually trumps state law, this is true only when the federal government—a government of limited powers—is entitled to pass a law in the specified area.

Chapter 10: Decisional Law

So far, we have discussed 'law' in the usual sense of the word, that is, laws passed by legislatures, statutes. But judges too have an important role to play in the development of law. Of course, court rulings have to be consistent with statute (unless the statute is unconstitutional), and unless a judge issues a ruling that is required by the constitution, the legislature can usually supersede a court decision if it disagrees.

Aside from simply implementing the wording of statutes as written, judges contribute in roughly three ways to the development and implementation of the law, and to that extent judges might be said to "make" law.

First, judges must fill in the interstices, that is, where there is some gap in the statute's coverage. Often a statute is silent, and its wording does not indicate how a specific case is meant to be decided. Even so, the judge still needs to rule; one side, or the other, must win the case. The judge may look at the legislative intent, as that can be discerned from the language of the statute itself or statements made by legislators at the time the statute was passed. For example, the tax laws treat gifts and profits from a business differently. We have to pay different rates of tax, depending on whether something is a gift or income from a business. A court may have to come up with various tests or criteria to decide how to make the distinction between "income" and a "gift." Courts are asked every day to interpret law and apply them to new factual situations never considered by the legislature that enacted the law. Courts can't refuse to do this: they *must* decide, one way or the other, whether the statute applies to the new or bizarre factual situation.

Second, as an extrapolation of the first situation, judges must come up with ways to apply statutes when the statute is silent. For example, a statute might make copyright infringement illegal but the courts may need to come up with a method to evaluate whether a new work takes enough from an old work to be termed an illegal copy. Just copying the general idea of a play or novel, for example, isn't enough to prove copyright infringement; but it doesn't *say* that in the copyright statute. Stopping a car at a sobriety checkpoint to see if the driver is drunk is generally not an "unreasonable" search and seizure, but of course the Fourth Amendment has no language on the issue. If a company breaches a promise on a web site that private information such as credit card numbers will be kept private, it's an "unfair trade practice" under the federal law that regulates the Federal Trade Commission—but there's nothing in the statute which actually says so.

Third, judges are often authorized by law to exercise their discretion and rule as they see fit, usually within certain bounds. For example, judges decide bail and sentence defendants after convictions at their discretion, although within certain limits. A judge cannot sentence a defendant to beyond the maximum term, and indeed usually can't sentence a defendant to the maximum term for no reason at all. A judge can't set bail at a billion dollars for someone who poses no risk of fleeing the jurisdiction. So, there are always limits to a judge's discretion. But within those limits, judges are free to decide. There are many areas in which judges are expected to exercise their discretion, and as those cases are reviewed by appellate courts and either affirmed or reversed, one can begin to discern the boundaries for the exercise of discretion, and the sorts of things judges are to consider as they exercise that discretion.

For example, in 'discovery disputes' judges are often asked to decide whether or not one side must, prior to trial, turn over certain evidence it has. The demanding party wants this "discovery," as we say. One side might have key documents, or a database of facts and figures, or a list of names of people or potential witnesses, or might have ten years' worth of accounting documents or backed-up emails. One side wants all the evidence it can get from the other side. But the responding side doesn't want to shoulder the time and monetary burden of finding, copying, and producing the evidence. A judge must weigh relevance versus burden, and decide the matter: How important is the evidence? Can it be obtained from somewhere else? Who should pay the costs? How much will it cost? Are the stakes in the case worth it—i.e. is this a case where $100 is involved or $1,000,000 is involved? All these factors are weighed. Judges exercise their discretion: perhaps they order the items produced, or not.

Another example: irrelevant evidence is not admissible at trial. Copies in place of original documents are not admissible, unless there's a good reason to think the copies are accurate. Reporting what someone else said outside the courtroom—hearsay—is usually not admissible. And so on. These are all rules of evidence. Now, one of these rules of evidence requires judges to weigh the relevance of evidence against the risk that the evidence might prejudice the jury. For example, assume we have a witness on the stand. The fact that he was convicted of fraud one year ago is relevant—the jury may use that prior conviction to consider whether the witness is trustworthy today. But if the witness is the defendant, the jury might also think that the fact that he was convicted of fraud last year means he's a crook and probably did the assault he's charged with now. That's the *prejudicial* effect of letting in the prior conviction. Should the judge allow mention of the past conviction because it's relevant to the defendant's credibility, or should the judge keep it out because it might bias the jury and is prejudicial? The judge exercises his discretion, using certain factors which he can discern from appellate opinions that have discussed the problem.

Indeed, in all these areas a judge will often find guidance in opinions of appellate courts. A judge might not be able to tell from a statute whether an apparently new situation is covered, but after reading ten opinions on a variety of different scenarios, the judge might have a very good idea of how to think about the issue and what to do in his particular case. Sometime the appellate opinions conflict with each other, in which case the judge either (1) follows the court of appeals that governs him, or

(2) if there is no such opinion, follows the one that seems to make the most sense.

As opinions are generated by the various courts of appeals, both federal and state, a body of law in effect develops. Some opinions are reversed or overturned, others are criticized, and some form the basis for further extrapolation in later opinions. There is a constant debate and discussion among judges, dead and alive, which creates its own traditions, accepted truths and rules, and modes of legal analysis. In many situations, this tradition is the law on which a judge must rely most heavily.

Chapter 11: Judges

Judges take an oath of office, which includes an oath to uphold the Constitution of the United States and (for state judges) the state constitution. They are obliged to follow the law, without regard to whether they like it or not. Their personal views on what the law should be are irrelevant. The views of the public on what the law ought to be are irrelevant. Judges must decide cases without regard to public clamor, or what they believe might be a popular decision. They must follow the law as they understand it, whether that law is found in a constitution, a statute, or in the opinions of courts above them in the hierarchy, such as the Supreme Court.

Judges do not have to follow the law as announced by a court which is not in that hierarchy, although those opinions might well be worth reading, as they may be persuasive. The "hierarchy" here means those courts higher up the ladder: for example, a federal district court in San Francisco is in the area governed by the Ninth Circuit and must follow the decisions of the Ninth Circuit Court of Appeals, but does not have to follow the decisions of the Seventh Circuit, which sits in Chicago and is responsible for a collection of Midwestern states. A state judge has to follow the opinions of his state's court of appeal, and of course his supreme court, but generally does not have to follow the decisions of federal courts or of judges in other states. All judges must follow the law as stated by the U.S. Supreme Court.

If the governing law clearly requires a certain result, then the judge must implement that result, even if the judge thinks it's unfair, morally wrong, or unjust. This is why some judges say their business is not to do justice—which may mean very different things to different people—but to follow the law. A judge cannot shade the law, or equivocate in his rulings, because he personally dislikes the result. A judge who did that would be violating his oath and be lawless, just as surely as a criminal who breaks the law. But a judge who violates the law can be far more dangerous than a criminal who steals a car: a lawless judge may create enormous damage in a large number of cases, and destroy people's confidence in the justice system.

There are indeed situations in which judges are asked to do things, or must rule a certain way according to law, which can be very difficult for the judge. The U.S. Supreme Court's Justice Kennedy, agreeing that the First Amendment protected a person's right to burn the flag as protest, famously wrote, "The hard fact is that sometimes we must make decisions we do not like. We make them because they are right, right in the sense that the law and the Constitution, as we see them, compel the result." Some judges who are observant Catholics may be obliged to protect a woman's constitutional right to have an abortion. Judges who personally are against the death penalty may be required to sentence a defendant to death. Some years ago, the federal system included Sentencing Guidelines, which in fact operated as sentencing requirements, taking most of the discretion away from judges in terms of which sentences to hand down. The Guidelines were thought by many to be particularly tough on certain kinds of drug offenses, even where the amount of drugs at stake was very little, and even where there was no prior criminal history. Some judges balked at handing down very long sentences in situations in which they thought it was grossly unfair. Some judges believed they simply could not do it. They resigned from the bench. That is precisely the appropriate thing to do: if for whatever reason a judge finds she in good conscience is unable to follow the law as she understands it, she must resign.

What Judges Do

Judges decide what the law is, and based on that law they make decisions on who wins and loses cases. If they preside at a bench trial (without a jury), they decide what the facts are, as well. Judges preside at trials, making the proceedings orderly and fair. They rule on objections to evidence, ensuring that juries hear exclusively evidence which is relevant and qualified under the Evidence Code. In criminal cases, judges set bail, which relates to the amount of money the defendant needs to put up to obtain his release, and sentences defendants who are found guilty of crimes. Legal issues are presented to judges in a wide variety of circumstances, many of which are described in more detail later in this book as we trace a typical criminal and a typical civil case.

These legal issues are usually presented to judges by way of a motion. A motion is a request for a judge to do something. It can be made in writing or orally in court. Motions usually state what the relevant facts are; sometimes it's obvious what those facts are. The motion might refer the judge to pertinent appellate cases, or statutes, and then make arguments based on that law, as well as arguments based on practicalities. Some motions are simple and some are complex. A simple motion might be made in the middle of trial, say an objection to evidence, and consist of just two words: "Objection, hearsay." This is a request to the judge that the evidence be excluded. Complex motions can involve a stack of paper literally five feet high, e.g., a motion for summary judgment. Motions for summary judgment are filed in civil cases, and ask the judge to rule that because the facts cannot be disputed, there's no reason to have a trial and judgment should immediately be entered for the party that brought the motion. Often those motions enclose and discuss an enormous amount of evidence all in an effort to show there are no facts in dispute.

There are then roughly three sorts of roles judges have. First, they are neutral umpires making sure the agreed-on rules of the game are followed. Second, judges determine and apply the law. Third, judges ensure justice is done by behaving in a way that creates confidence in the system. "Justice" in this senses does not precisely mean that the final result in a case is or is not 'just.' Rather, it refers to the process, *how* the case is handled. If people believe they have been heard, that they were given a fair shake, that rules were applied the same way to both sides, that the judge read the legal materials and thought about the case and did her best to render the decision required by law, then even if they lose they will have confidence in the system; they will believe that in general the system is 'just.' Judges are directly responsible for this, and must act at all times (both in their private and public life) to further public confidence in the justice system.

How Judges Get the Job

Judges come from a wide variety of backgrounds, but almost all of them have been lawyers. With some exceptions, trial judges are culled from the ranks of lawyers, and appellate judges are culled from the trial judges. Justices on the Supreme Court often are appointed from the Courts of Appeals in both the federal and state systems, but there have been many notable examples of Supreme Court justices who have never been judges before, such as U.S. Supreme Court Chief Justice Earl Warren (Governor of California), Justice William O. Douglas (head of the Securities & Exchange Commission), and Justice Holmes (professor at a law school). Federal judges can become state judges and state judges can become federal judges.

In the federal system, judges are appointed by the President of the United States and confirmed by the U.S. Senate. This is true of all federal judges, from the trial courts to the U.S. Supreme Court. Federal judges are guaranteed a term for life under Article III of the U.S. Constitution, unless they are impeached by the House of Representatives and convicted by the Senate, in which case they are removed. There have been very, very few impeachments of federal judges.

In the California state system trial judges (who are on the Superior Court) run for office every six years, and in the case of a vacancy, the Governor appoints. As noted above, this in practice means that most judges are first appointed by the Governor. Appellate justices on the intermediate appellate courts and the state supreme court are nominated by the

Governor and approved by the Commission on Judicial Appointments. They have 12-year terms. The Commission on Judicial Appointments has three members: the Chief Justice of the state, the Attorney General, and the presiding justice of the appeal court in question.

Every judge has a unique story of how he or she came to the bench, and the reason he thinks he was able to get the job. For some, it was having good contacts with the President or Governor, perhaps being politically active. For others, it was preeminence in their profession, being held in esteem by fellow members of the bar. Because Senators have a powerful role in having the President nominate judges, many federal judges have a history of having good connections with a Senator. Some governors have preferred to appoint state prosecutors, others have been open to lawyers from prominent law firms and public defenders. The age of judges on their first appointment ranges from their thirties to the sixties. Some governors care very much that their appointee come from the same political party, others do not. Some judges have had wide and diverse legal experience before they came to the bench and others have not: their first taste of a criminal or civil case might come on their first day as a judge. For most new judges, the first few years are a steep learning curve.

Let's contrast the process of getting appointed as a federal or state trial judge.

In the federal system, one typically must have one's name put forward by one's Senator. Senators have very different ways to screen candidates: some have a committee that tries to pick the most qualified; other Senators do the work on a more personal basis, appointing people with whom they are familiar. A variety of types of information may be required from the candidate. Different administrations have handled matters differently. Some require an interview at the White House by the President's staff, while others do not. In every case the FBI conducts a background check. The America Bar Association generally issues a rating of the candidate's qualifications. If the President approves, the name is sent by the President to the Senate, where hearings are held on the candidate's qualifications. If a majority of the Senate approves, the person is confirmed and becomes a judge.

In the California state system, a candidate fills out a very lengthy questionnaire about his background. The governor usually has an Appointments Secretary, who reviews the questionnaires and, following the Governor's instructions, decides whose name should be put forward or "nominated." The names of nominated candidates are then sent to the Judicial Evaluation and Nominations (JNE) commission, made up of lawyers who have volunteered for the job. This commission sends out questionnaires to sometimes hundreds of people who might know the candidate, and it interviews each candidate at some length. Based on that information, the JNE commission (informally pronounced as the 'jenny' commission) issues a rating from very 'highly qualified' through 'not qualified.' The Governor may ignore the recommendations, although it can be somewhat embarrassing to appoint someone who received a "not qualified" rating from the JNE commission. Usually the Governor's office nominates at least a few people for each opening; and based on all the information collected, the Governor picks one and appoints him or her to the bench.

State trial judges generally find out they have been appointed with a phone call from the Governor's Appointments Secretary. This is remembered as one of the best moments of the judge's life.

Judges are generally happy in their job, despite the very high stress levels. They must deal with having too many cases while receiving relatively low salaries. (State trial judges make about as much as a second year associate in a large law firm; at the time of this writing, federal trial judges make even less.) They must handle a wide variety of issues, some of the them complex and difficult, and deal with lawyers of (to be polite!) varied skill levels. Judges are after all a self selecting group, making a career choice late in life often with a fairly good sense of what the judicial life will be like. They understand that their professional life will be isolated, and that their personal life is also likely to contract severely. They are under a variety of constraints, outlined below, including the fact that they cannot speak to anyone except other judges about their work. Indeed, California judges are barred from commenting on *any* pending case, anywhere in the world. But judges appreciate the public service role they have, the opportunity to devote their entire career to a single goal of following the law, unadulterated by politics or answering to a "boss" or business considerations or the needs of a firm's partners or indeed anyone's needs. American judges are part of a tradition that stretches back over a thousand years into England's legal history, the front line in the constant struggle for a peaceful, lawful and constitutionally based society.

Constraints on the Power of Judges

Much media coverage suggests an "unelected" judiciary severed from constraints, judges free to rule as pique and whim carry them. But the rhetoric often plays off public ignorance, not the least of which ignores the fact that many judges *are* elected and subject to challenge at the polls.

Aside from attorneys and judges, few know much about the courts and the constraints under which judges operate. Instead, most citizens' information comes from television shows displaying personality-driven rough justice, or sound bite reports on the results of a case. As portrayed, these judges do often sound unprincipled. Real courts seem to be a distant land, where decisions are made behind closed doors, judges are clothed in impenetrable black robes, and the occasional Latin phrase enlivens the cloistered debate.

Too, the essential emphasis in this country on an *independent* judiciary confounds this picture, because some take that "independence" to mean uninhibited whim, a license to impose judges' personal sense of morality, their own sense of right and wrong, as well as political, cultural and religious views.

That is a false picture. The truth is that judges are subject to a series of overt and profound constraints. There is room for discretion, but these constraints tend to guide judges' decisions in a way that is generally unknown or poorly understood by the public.

Let us take as a model the rules and constraints for California state judges. California is the world's fifth or sixth largest economy, and has the largest judicial system in the world, with about 1800 bench officers (judges and so-called 'subordinate judicial officers' such as commissioners who are hired by judges). California is, therefore, a typical or at least dominant example.

The trial courts serve as a good example because virtually all the business of the judiciary is handled at the trial level. Relatively few cases are decided by the courts of appeal, and almost none by the supreme court. While the supreme courts—those of states, or the federal supreme court in Washington D.C. which takes cases originating from both the states and the federal trial courts—make the "big" (at least final) decisions, most of us are personally affected and have to live with the decisions of lower level trial courts.

In California, trial court judges take office in two ways: some are elected in contested races, like politicians. Most are first appointed by the governor to fill a vacancy, and then they may be challenged within the next few years at the polls. The decisions of trial judges are reviewed by the intermediate courts of appeal, and the decisions of those appellate courts are in turn reviewable by the California Supreme Court. "Reviewable" here means the Supreme Court usually chooses whether or not to take the case; and it rarely does. The appellate judges and supreme court judges (known as "justices") are appointed by the governor, but may be recalled, or thrown out of office, by the voters. In 1986 three California Supreme Court justices including Chief Justice Rose Bird were recalled by the voters, and lost their jobs. It was a rare event, but it happened.

The judgments of trial judges are of course reviewable by the appellate courts, where a panel of three judges must determine if an error of law was made. Trial judges, however, do much more than issue those sorts of final judgments. An almost infinite number of interim rulings also are made, such as setting cases for trial, ruling on evidentiary objections, seating jurors over the objection of a lawyer, setting time limits, and so on- -- which are not reviewed by a higher court as a matter of right. But there's a safety valve even here: any decision by a trial court may be the subject of a "writ" proceeding. This means the appellate court in an extraordinary case can reach down and reverse almost any decision of a trial judge. About one to two percent of writ petitions are granted.

The Supreme Court does not have to accept petitions from the decisions of the intermediate appellate courts, and so practically speaking the last word in almost all cases is from that court of appeal. But even when stopping there, cases will have been evaluated by four judges in total. Probably more importantly, the trial judges *know* that their decisions will be reviewed by their superiors, and no one likes to be reversed. So too, the court of appeal justices know that their Supreme Court colleagues may review their work, and the mere possibility of review is a check in its own right.

Anyone—lawyers, members of the public, litigants—may complain to the Commission on Judicial Performance (CJP) about a judge. The CJP won't look at suggestions of legal error—that a judge got the law wrong— but does look at allegations of misconduct, and in a serious case will remove the judge. Lesser infractions receive private or public reprovals. Public reprovals or admonishments can be difficult to explain in the next election cycle. Avoiding notice by the CJP is a powerful incentive for judges.

There is an enormous range of behavior which qualifies as misconduct. Obvious are biased actions, or those displaying prejudice or taking money from litigants. Rude, demeaning treatment of lawyers and litigants also will get a judge into deep trouble. Using the judicial title for private or personal advantage—such as displaying the judicial badge at a police stop, or on letterhead when complaining to one's plumber about the bill—are also abuses. The list is a very, very long one. Judges are subject to gift limits. There are bars on certain payments for travel, appearances at political rallies, fundraising, and so on. Both the California Supreme Court, through its approval of the canons of judicial ethics, and the legislature through laws, define judicial misconduct. Quite aside from discipline, failure to adhere to some of these obligations will result in criminal penalties, and a few result in an automatic forfeiture of the office.

The canons on judicial ethics block a series of behaviors by both judges and their families, and compel disclosure or disqualification where the judge might be perceived as biased (even if in fact the judge isn't biased at all).

Judges, like other public officials, must report their gifts, paid travel, and investments every year on a form available to the public. The report is made under penalty of perjury, so false statements are a crime. A separate state commission is responsible for enforcing these rules and fining miscreants.

Critically, judges have the central constraint of public scrutiny. True, this is a public which does not often exercise its raw power of control and accountability through that observation. But courtrooms are open, and case files can be read by anyone. Judges have to explain their final decisions in written statements. Except in the most extraordinary cases, judges cannot interfere with a media report and cannot seal a record.

The way judges are selected, too, operates as a severe constraint. Those elected are known in the community, and by definition enjoy widespread support. Those appointed in California have endured remarkable scrutiny of their past while under consideration for appointment. Lawyers and judges they have known over decades of legal practice are asked to comment, and the JNE commission investigates and eventually interviews the finalists at length. Local bar associations often weigh in and conduct interviews, as well as poll their members. The Governor's office completes the process with credit and other checks, and conducts an in-depth interview of the "final" finalists.

Education and peer expectations also operate as constraints. Upon appointment, new judges are sent off for a week of formal education and training in ethics, bias, courtroom control, and related issues. Then within the first year or two in office, they must attend a two week judicial college which expands on these subjects and moves into other areas as well. Every three years they must take another series of courses in judicial ethics. Every time they take on a substantial new assignment, they must take a course on the new area.

Most judges are on courts with many colleagues; in San Francisco, for example, there are about 65 judges and commissioners. Judges are by law subject to the direction of the presiding judge, who in turn is elected by the judges in any particular court. The "PJ," as he is called, not only assigns cases, parcels out vacation time, and supervises the administration of the court, but also can and does look into suggestions that judges have departed from acceptable behavior.

In their totality all these constraints operate to create a web of restriction with a central underlying theme: judges are public servants, but they are not subject to the direction of any given segment of the public. That is, they are servants of the *whole* public. There is only one group who actually can influence judges, and that is the whole public, acting through either its legislature or passage of a statewide ballot measure. The independent judiciary is independent, that is, from all outside influence except the influence of law. This is fundamental to the system of checks and balances laid out in the U.S. Constitution.

These constraints do not always work, of course. As with any profession, there are some who break the rules. The CJP's Annual Report includes a Case Summaries section which makes for fascinating, if somewhat prurient, reading. But the instances of misconduct are rare. For example in 2004 the CJP handled 1080 complaints; 27 resulted in disciplinary procedures (including two judges who resigned or retired).

It will be objected: this is not the whole story. Surely there are decisions not hemmed in by precedent, or which are in effect unreviewable: when a court can decide a matter either way, where neither the CJP nor the court of appeals nor the PJ will interfere. The point is accurate: despite all the constraints that have been outlined here, there are still some areas in which judges must simply do what they think is best. Indeed, the trial court judge's day is filled with such decisions; they can come every minute or two. This is why we *have* judges; these choices are the essence of judging. If there were no such decisions we could use computers to operate the justice system. Some decisions such as admitting or refusing evidence at trial, ordering evidence to be produced, imposing sanctions, seating jurors, setting bail, setting trial dates, and so on, all are effectively committed to the 'sound discretion' of the trial judge. In all these cases, a judge *could go either way* and still be right: honest, fair, impartial, and lawful. It does not follow that one of these decisions is "right" and the other is "wrong"—i.e., the result of personal prejudice, bias, whim or pique, or the consequence of an otherwise hidden social agenda.

The decision in a given case may not be assured, or common among all judges of a court. But the series of constraints outlined above do assure us of something more fundamental. They assure us that the judge will likely reach a decision (1) within a rang of *reasonable alternatives*, (2) based on *set procedures* and (3) considering only a *prescribed series of factors*. These are the circumstances designed to assure justice: i.e., decisions which are both consistent with the law, and are essentially the result of fair procedures.

Few aside from judges and lawyers really know what these set procedures are, or the factors on which judges base their decisions. Few know how the courts operate, and from that perspective it is understandable that some decisions can appear groundless, the seeming result of whim and caprice. As one respondent in a 1999 national survey said, "The average person doesn't know the law, and is more afraid of it than anything else. The law is difficult to understand, and there needs to be a general understanding, but it is not shared by the people of the courts. I don't think that what the people think and what the courts think is the same." (We have a citation to the survey in the Resources section of this book.) The same study noted that 44% thought courts were out of touch with the community (minority groups were much more likely to agree). The study also confirmed that many people obtained their information about the justice system from reality TV shows such as "Judge Judy." Over half sometimes (32%) or frequently (19%) got their information about courts from TV dramas.

So we are full circle. Much of the rhetoric suggesting that the courts are 'too' independent, deciding cases by untrammeled whim, may be a function of ignorance. There is a failure of the public to know their judicial systems, a failure of the courts and the legal profession to tell them about it, and a failure of the educational system to ensure the knowledge is transmitted. This is an ignorance which, in this of all nations, should not be tolerated. The United States is founded on the rule of law and the almost sacred primacy of the written Constitution. This is effective as long as we have a independent branch of government whose job description is, in short, to uphold that Constitution. But the operation of this third branch, like the others, depends on an informed citizenry.

Chapter 12: A Story about a Civil Case

Here, we explain in some detail the hypothetical civil case introduced at the beginning of this book. Later we'll follow the details of the companion criminal case. Before we start, a refresher on the participants.

Ervin Johnson is the driver of the truck who crashed into the car containing Harry Pitt and Kim Hollings. Hollings was killed, and the civil suit against Johnson was brought by her parents (on her behalf) and by Pitt who was seriously injured in the accident. Don Simon is the lawyer for Pitt and Hollings in the civil case. Karin Kramer is the lawyer for Johnson in the civil case.

The lawyers in the *criminal* case are the assistant District Attorney (for the People of the State of California), and the assistant Public Defender (for Johnson, appointed because Johnson could not afford to hire a lawyer for his criminal case).

Below is a chart of who was involved in these cases:

	Lawyers in the civil case	Lawyers in the criminal case	Clients
Plaintiff	Don Simon	The assistant district attorney ("DA")	Kim Hollings and Harry Pitt
Defendant	Karin Kramer	The assistant public defender ("PD")	Ervin Johnson

Here's what happened in the civil case:

After a period of mourning following the burial of Kim Hollings, her parents spoke to the Pitt family and they decided that they wanted to sue

Johnson, whom they held at fault in the accident. Both the Pitt and Hollings families had very high medical and other expenses as a result of the accident, and they felt that in addition to any criminal penalties Johnson might suffer in his criminal case, he should be responsible for the medical costs and lost income, too. The two families couldn't afford a lawyer, but they had heard of Don Simon who agreed to take the case on a contingency—he'd charge them nothing (except for some court costs). If Simon won the case, he would take 1/3 of the recovery, that is, 1/3 of whatever the jury awarded. If Simon lost the case, he would receive no payment at all for his work on the case. Simon, in short, was making a bet that he could win the case, and that the amount he would recover was enough to compensate him for the time he would put into the case.

The Complaint is Filed

About five months after the accident, Simon filed the complaint in the Superior Court. This was a three page document which very briefly laid out the facts, charged Ervin Johnson with driving while under the influence, and having as a result crashed his truck into the car containing Pitt and Hollings. Johnson was accused in the complaint of negligence, and with acting in reckless disregard of the life of others. The complaint asked for ten million dollars in compensatory damages and a hundred million in punitive damages. Simon didn't really know how much to ask for, but he had to make some rough, preliminary estimate. Simon arranged to have a copy of the complaint personally served on Johnson. This means he got a company which specializes in this sort of service to hand a copy of the complaint, in person, to Johnson. That way, it was clear Johnson was "on notice"--i.e., knew about—the filing of the complaint.

The Role of Insurance

Normally people involved in a civil case have to find and hire their own lawyers. This is true whether one is bringing the case (a plaintiff) or defending against someone else's suit (a defendant). But sometimes an insurance company will supply the lawyer. This is called "providing a defense," and is often the situation in cases involving car accidents, because in most states everyone who owns a car has to have at least some insurance coverage. Usually, the insurance company will not only pay a settlement (or verdict) for a case when the insured person is sued, but also supply a lawyer. Of course, the insurance company need only pay out on a settlement (or jury verdict) up to the maximum as set forth in the insurance policy (called the policy limit), and the insured will have to pay anything over those limits. But providing a defense is a valuable benefit of these policies, and in our hypothetical case here, is the only reason Johnson was able to have a lawyer defend him in the case brought by Hollings and Pitt.

Juries are instructed that whether someone has insurance or not is totally irrelevant, and they are almost never told if any of the parties in a lawsuit has insurance.

The Answer is Filed

As soon as Johnson actually received his copy of the Complaint, the clock was running. Johnson had thirty days to answer the complaint. If he didn't, Simon would be able to go into court and get a default judgment, which would mean Simon would win the case automatically since the court would think Johnson wasn't contesting anything. Filing a document called an "Answer" is the signal that a defendant is contesting the case. Johnson had to find a lawyer, and in a hurry. Twenty days later Karin Kramer agreed to represent Johnson, but at this point there were only ten days left in which to file the Answer. Kramer called Simon, and the two agreed that Kramer could have another thirty days to answer. Just before the new deadline, Kramer filed an Answer for Johnson. That Answer denied the allegations in the Complaint, and went on to list a series of affirmative defenses. Affirmative defenses are statement of legal principles that the defendant thinks will win him the case. For example, there are time limits after which people can't sue each other. In California, you can't sue for breach of a written contract more than four years after the breach. So if the case were filed five years after the breach, the defendant might have an "affirmative defense" that more than four years had passed.

In this case against Johnson, one affirmative defense was that the time period for filing the complaint had passed. Another one was that some third party or the plaintiffs Hollings and Pitt were really responsible for the accident, and so on and so forth. Most of the Answer was legal routine, or boilerplate, using words commonly found in Answers.

Motion to Dismiss, and Demurrer

Kramer actually had had a choice when the deadline came up to file an Answer. She could have filed a different paper, instead. She could have demurred to the complaint (as we say in state court). A demurrer is a motion which asks the court to dismiss the case right away on the grounds that the complaint "fails to state a cause of action." Demurrers try to argue that even if everything alleged in the complaint is true, the plaintiff still could not possibly win.

For example, suppose a plaintiff wrote in his complaint that some contract was breached by a defendant, and it was obvious that the plaintiff had nothing to do with the contract, e.g. he hadn't signed it, nor was he to benefit from it. The defendant would file a demurrer stating that the plaintiff had no right to win anything, even if the defendant *had* breached some contract.

In this case, Kramer knew that there was no good chance the demurrer would win, and would only drive up the cost of litigation, so she simply filed the Answer.

Discovery

As soon as the Answer was on file, the two sides began to pepper each other with discovery demands. These demands are designed to find out what sort of information the other side has, so that by the time of trial there is no surprise, and so that each side knows how strong a case the other side has, which in theory should allow the case to settle on reasonable terms without the need actually to go to trial. Discovery also helps determine who the best witnesses will be, and to get a good sense of what they would say at trial. In discovery, one also can have witnesses answer questions in official recorded sessions—recorded by either video tape, or by a court reporter who prints up the questions and answers—and the recorded session can be used at trial, instead of having to call the witnesses.

Discovery can be expensive, very expensive. In fact, in most civil cases the costs of discovery account for almost all the costs. It takes a lot of time for lawyers, and their staff, to draft questions, review the responses, and argue in court about whether the responses are adequate. It takes a lot of time to ask for, collect, and review the sometimes thousands of documents that might be involved in a case. Below, we map out the various ways in which "discovery" is conducted. Most of these are time consuming.

In each case, the lawyers have to consider whether the costs of discovery are worth the possible benefits. Often the lawyers will disagree and the judge will have to consider the balance of benefits vs. costs when resolving discovery disputes, as we'll see later.

There are four main types of discovery: interrogatories, requests for admission, depositions, and document requests.

Interrogatories

Interrogatories are simply questions. The other side has to answer them under oath, in writing. The answers can be used at trial. In this case, Simon sent a set of interrogatories to Kramer for Johnson to answer. They included such questions as this: Did you drive a truck at 3.20 A.M. on the night of the accident? Had you been drinking, and if so, what did you drink? What was the name of the bartender? Who else was at the bar while you were there? Have you been previously convicted of any crimes? Did your truck get repaired after the accident and if so, by whom, and how much did it cost?

Kramer also sent a set of interrogatories to Simon, to be answered by Pitt and the parents of Hollings. Questions included these: Had you (Pitt or Hollings) been drinking at the time of the accident? Do you know the names of anyone who saw the accident, or who saw whether the light was red or green? What are your medical bills so far and how much do you expect they will be in the future? What is the basis for your estimate about future medical costs? Did you lose any income from not working as a result of the accident? How much? Provide all contact information for any doctors who tested you.

And so on.

Both sides reviewed the interrogatories with which they had been served. They answered some of the questions. They objected to some of the questions, saying the questions were overly burdensome, and it would take too much effort to answer them. The lawyers exchanged sometimes unpleasant letters complaining about the other side's replies, but they resolved most of the disputes. Finally after Simon refused to provide all the names of the treating doctors (he thought it was too much of a burden and that Kramer could get the information herself from the hospital), Kramer filed a discovery motion, that is, a motion to compel further responses to the interrogatories. Simon filed an opposition to the motion, and Kramer filed a reply memorandum. They had a hearing in front of a judge, who ruled that Simon had to turn over whatever information he had, but that he didn't have to do any further investigation to get more information. The judge gave Simon ten days to get that done. In all, it had been six months since the interrogatories had been served on the other side to get that response. Later, after they had a chance to get a series of documents related to the case (see below, Document Demands), each side sent the other another set of interrogatories, and they went through the entire process all over again.

Requests for Admission

A party also can ask the other side to admit something is true, all to allow the case to focus on what is truly in dispute. Responses to these Requests can be used at trial. Here, Simon sent requests that Johnson admit that he owned the truck, that he'd been driving it, that he had at least 5 beers, that he crashed into the Pitt-Hollings car, and so on. Simon thought Johnson would admit at least those statements.

Depositions

Depositions are live question and answer sessions. They are statements under oath, just like trial testimony. One can take the deposition of a party in the case, or of so-called "third parties," that is, people other than those directly involved in the case. One can also take the deposition of experts. Simon wanted to take the deposition of Johnson, of course, as well as the third party bartender who could talk about what Johnson had to drink that night. Kramer took the depositions of doctors who attended Pitt and Hollings, and also took Pitt's deposition.

Depositions are usually taken from two different kinds of witnesses, i.e., so-called "percipient" witnesses—people who saw what happened—and experts. Experts are informed of various facts and provide opinions, based on their expertise, education, and training. Sometimes, a case will come down to a battle of experts, and the jury has to decide which is the most convincing. In this case, both sides hired experts to give opinions on the cause of the accident. Simon, on behalf of Pitt and Hollings, had an expert who would testify that the accident must have been caused by the truck slamming into the side of the victim's car, and that the truck driver (Johnson) must have seen the car in advance and should have braked, but never did. Kramer, on behalf of Johnson, also hired an expert. Kramer's expert looked at the tire marks on the road, made some measurements and calculations, and had an opinion that the Pitt-Hollings car had been going too fast through the light, and if they had been going at the speed limit they would have had time to stop, so the accident was in that sense caused by Hollings.

Each lawyer took the deposition of the other side's experts. They also took depositions of the doctors, who were in one sense percipient witnesses—they'd seen the condition of Hollings and Pitt—and also provided some expert testimony on the causes of the injuries. Simon also hired an accident reconstruction expert, who made an animated video showing the accident as it happened—at least, as Simon and his other expert contended the accident must have happened.

Kramer also took the deposition of this accident reconstruction expert, in order to find out what he would say about the assumption he made as he created the video. Kramer did this to accumulate information for cross examination at trial. She also know that, if she wanted to, she could probably cross examine this expert at trial on the basis of his deposition testimony. If he contradicted, at trial, what he said in the deposition, Kramer would be able to confront him in front of the jury with the earlier statement.

Document Demands

Parties in lawsuits send out demands for documents. Obviously Kramer wanted to see all the medical records, and all documents which had been inspected by any of Simon's experts. Simon wanted similar documents from Kramer. Kramer also wanted all documents that supported Pitt's and Hollings' claims for lost wages.

Kramer also issued a subpoena for documents to a third party— Pitt's employer, the local supermarket, asking for every document associated with Pitt, all document concerning calculation of leave, vacation, and payment of wages, deductions for taxes, and every other piece of paper Kramer could think of that might possibly relate to the amount of money Pitt might have lost as a result of the accident. The lawyer for the third party supermarket refused, claiming the request was overly burdensome, and the two brought the matter in front of the judge. The judge agreed that all the materials were, to some extent, relevant, or might lead to the discovery of some relevant evidence. But the supermarket provided testimony that it would cost them a hundred thousand dollars to find every single paper requested by Kramer. So the judge told Kramer that he would allow the discovery, but Kramer (Kramer's client) would have to pay for it. Kramer rethought her position and specified just a few documents she really needed.

Objections

Lawyers can object to questions, requests for admissions, interrogatories, and other demands made as part of the pre-trial "discovery" process. If they do not agree on what is reasonable and proper to ask, they prepare written motions and oppositions to those motions for a judge, and the judge decides the issue.

For example, in our case, objections were made to the deposition of Pitt. Lawyer Karin Kramer asked when Pitt had first told his lawyer that he thought Johnson had gone through a red light. Simon objected, and Kramer thought better of the question, because it might invade the attorney-client communication privilege, which is a law that keeps secret the conversations between attorneys and their lawyers. But if the lawyers had not been able to resolve their differences, the lawyer who wanted to ask the question would have been able to make a motion before the judge, and get a determination whether the witnesses must answer the question. Usually judges will order questions must be answered if they are relevant, not a waste of time or designed to harass the witness, and if the question doesn't compromise a privilege not to testify. For example, after Simon told Kramer he wanted to take the deposition of Ervin Johnson, Kramer responded by letter refusing to produce Johnson. The basis for her refusal was that Johnson's criminal DUI case was still pending in state court, and he should not have to make any statements that might tend to incriminate him. Kramer cited the Fifth Amendment to the U.S. Constitution, which guarantees that a defendant can not be made to incriminate himself. Simon agreed, and did not send out a notice for Johnson's deposition until after his criminal case was over. By that time, Johnson was in state prison, and that's where they took the deposition—in a meeting room set aside by the prison for meetings with lawyers.

Motion for Summary Judgment

After Kramer thought she had more or less all the evidence she was going to get from Simon, she brought a motion for summary judgment. She attached excerpts from the depositions she had taken, and some of the interrogatory replies from Pitt and Hollings. She also attached a series of documents prepared by her expert, plus a sworn statement from her expert. All told, the papers submitted to the judge were about six inches thick. Kramer's argument was based on her expert's opinion that the accident was in fact caused by Pitt's going too fast, and not stopping after Pitt had been in a position to see Johnson's truck coming at him. Kramer argued that no reasonable jury could possibly find Johnson was really the cause of the accident, and therefore no jury trial was needed. Johnson should now win the case brought against him, and Pitt and Hollings should get nothing.

Of course, Simon opposed the motion. He argued that Kramer's expert's opinion was based on questionable data, and said that a jury was not likely to agree with all the factual assumptions made by Kramer's expert. In addition, Simon had his own expert, who disagreed with Kramer's expert. The judge decided that a reasonable jury could go either way, and so the motion for summary judgment had to be denied. The case would have to go to a jury.

Settlement and Settlement Conferences

Most cases actually settle before trial. Around 90% of cases get resolved before trial through a combination of settlement, summary judgment motions and other pretrial procedures. Sometimes the parties simply negotiate among themselves informally. This process can get started by a letter from one lawyer to another, a discussion at a meeting for a deposition, or a contact made when they're in court on some motion. Often a judge will ask the parties if they've had a chance to talk about settling the case.

Sometimes it is hard for a lawyer to begin settlement discussions, and some lawyers think it is a sign of weakness to start those discussions, although it's not. Lawyers know that the earlier they settle the case, the less money they'll spend preparing for a trial that probably won't take place. Courts usually require the parties to have a settlement conference, to get the ball rolling and make it clear that the court expects the parties to think seriously about settlement. Sometimes the local bar association provides facilities for other lawyers to help out by talking to the parties about settlement at a set time and place.

Many judges hold mandatory settlement conferences with the lawyers some time after most of the discovery process is over, and the judges talk to the parties about settlement. The case might not settle that day, but the discussion might lead to settlement later. It doesn't cost anything to engage in these discussions, except for the money one might be spending on the lawyer. The services of the court and of the bar association are free. In federal court in San Francisco and elsewhere, the courts try to get the parties to take a good hard look very early in the life of a case, when settlement will make the most difference in terms of saving the costs of litigation. In some cases that works. In other cases the lawyers say they need to know about the other side's case—they need to engage in discovery—before they can have a good sense of what the case should settle for.

The two parties sometimes handle their case quite apart from the court system. If they want to, they can hire an expert in settlement to help them resolve their case. Of course, they have to pay that person's fee, which can be very, very high for some of the best known settlement (or "mediation") experts. Unlike judges who have limited time to try to settle any given cases, hired mediation experts will generally give the case as much time as the parties desire, since they are being paid to do so. Some of the mediators are retired judges, some are lawyers. Mediators only help the parties to reach an agreement between themselves. They do not have the power to force the parties to agree to anything, or actually to *decide* the result of the case. The term "Alternative Dispute Resolution" or ADR is used to describe these sorts of outside-of-court proceedings.

People also can agree to arbitrate their cases, which means hiring an arbitrator to *decide* the case. This too is a form of ADR, and again, the parties usually have to pay a fee to the arbitrator for these services. In our case, Kramer asked Simon to agree to take the case out of the court system and submit it to an arbitrator, but Simon refused. He thought he'd have a better chance of a very high award with a jury. In addition, he didn't want to spend a lot on money on a hired mediator, because the fees would come out of his pocket (his client couldn't afford it) and he didn't think there was much the mediator could help with in a case which Simon thought was essentially simple and straightforward.

Simon did try to resolve the case informally with Kramer, and the two lawyers exchanged a series of offers after the motion for summary judgment was denied. Simon pointed out that now nothing stood in the way of a jury trial, and he thought a jury would be upset about Johnson's drinking and driving, and would decide a hefty punitive damages award. Kramer replied that she expected the jury would think Pitt and Hollings were greedy, trying to hit a jackpot, and that her expert, who had testified in scores of trials with a lot of success, would probably convince the jury that Pitt and Hollings weren't entitled to anything at all. She said she wasn't afraid of a punitive damages award, because the jury would hear that Johnson wasn't worth much anyway, and didn't have the money to pay any large award. She was, she wrote, willing to settle the case for $200,000. Simon was holding out for millions of dollars. He declined the settlement offer from Kramer, and said he'd see her in court.

Getting Ready for Trial

The weeks leading up the trial were a nightmare for the lawyers. They had to make sure their witnesses were ready, not just for questions their own lawyers would ask, but for the questions to be asked by the other side. Legal issues had to be researched. They had to write up memoranda on the issues, as well as outlines of questions to ask, what the responses would be, and notes on which documents to ask which witnesses about. The lawyers had to research and consider the likely evidence issues that might come up. They had to be prepared to argue why their evidence should be heard by the jury, and why evidence from the other side should not. They reviewed all the depositions taken in the case, made summaries of those depositions, and further, made notes about which portions of the depositions they would try to get in front of the jury. All the evidence had to be sorted and organized, and all the witnesses had to understand what they would say about the evidence (such as documents). The lawyers considered what they'd be looking for in a jury, and what questions they wished to ask of the prospective jurors. They spoke to their friends and colleagues about the judge—how he conducted trials, how he tended to rule on certain issues, and so on. They outlined their opening statements, and practiced them. They also outlined their closing arguments, although of course these would likely be updated as the trial progressed. They hired companies to make enlargements of key documents, and Simon made sure his audio visual expert knew how to operate the machinery in court. He bought an extra light bulb and extension cord for the projector and had a back up plan in case the technology didn't work at all.

Trial

The Burden of Proof: By a Preponderance of the Evidence

Simon, on behalf of Pitt and Hollings, had brought the case. He represented the plaintiffs. So he had the burden of proving his case. The burden in civil cases is known as the "preponderance of the evidence" which means the jury should return a verdict for Simon's clients if the jury found that on balance the evidence tipped (50% plus) in favor of the plaintiffs. Otherwise, the verdict should go for Ervin Johnson, the defendant.

Judge ("Bench") vs. Jury Trial

When the day came for their trial, the lawyers went to the courtroom of the Presiding Judge, who knew which judges were available for trial that day. The Presiding Judge has many duties, and one of them is acting as a sort of traffic cop, sending cases to judges as they are available to handle them. The Presiding Judge ("PJ") in fact didn't have any judges that day, but knew one of his judges, Paul Zieff, would be available the next day. So the PJ told Simon and Kramer to go to Judge Zieff's courtroom the next morning. The lawyer's pulses were racing. Both were experienced lawyers, but it's nerve wracking every time a trial is about to start. Both went back to their offices to prepare for the next day. Kramer poured over the depositions, looking for bits she could use against the other side. Simon went for a long walk and tried to think about nothing at all. He was not entirely successful.

The next morning the lawyers showed up in Judge Zieff's courtroom, and he invited them back into his office, just off the courtroom. Judges' offices are known as "chambers." In chambers, the judge first asked about settlement. He spoke first with only Simon and Kramer, trying to assure himself that the parties really had had a serious discussion about resolving the case. He then brought in the clients, Johnson and Pitt, and the parents of Hollings. He spoke for a few minutes about the advantages of settlement, and urged them to consider some sort of compromise. Finally, the judge saw that the case would not settle, and he excused the clients. He went over this courtroom guidelines with the lawyers—where to stand when asking question, and how he supervised picking the jury, and a variety of other mechanical details. He asked the lawyers if they would waive their right to a jury trial and instead simply try the case to the judge—a "bench" trial. To avoid any appearance of impropriety, he said he didn't want to hear from either side on this subject unless they privately agreed to a bench trial and reported that back him. He excused the lawyers for lunch and told them they would pick the jury that afternoon.

Getting Called for Jury Service

The parties—Johnson on the one side, and Pitt and the Hollings family on the other—were about to pick a jury of twelve people, and two alternates. Jury alternates hear everything the panel of twelve hears, and are available in case one of the twelve gets sick or misses court for some other reason.

Where do juries come from? U.S. citizens have a legal obligation to be available for jury service. Names are selected at random, usually from voter registration and licensed driver lists. Those people may receive a jury summons in the mail. A summons is actually a court order, and it requires the person be available for jury service as of a given date. If someone refuses to attend, the court may issue a warrant for his arrest.

In some counties, people can call in, or check a web site, to see if in fact they are needed for jury service on the day they have been summoned. In other places, they come into court and wait to see if they are needed. In most counties in the State of California, for example, a person will serve "one day or one trial" which means they must be available for a day to see if they are called to a courtroom, and if not, their obligation is satisfied for the year. If they *are* called to a courtroom, it may take a few days to pick a jury, but they generally will not be sent to another courtroom if they are excused from the courtroom they are called to first.

Potential jurors wait in what is usually called the jury assembly room. When a judge is ready to pick a jury, his clerk calls the jury assembly room, and a certain number of people are sent to that courtroom. Usually, about 60-80 potential jurors are sent at a time.

Jury Selection

After lunch, the lawyers appeared in Judge Zieff's courtroom at 1:30 in the afternoon. Within the next twenty minutes, the room filled with 80 citizens from the county, all of whom had been sent to Judge Zieff's courtroom from the court's jury assembly room where they had been waiting earlier that day.

Judge Zieff welcomed the panel. He talked about the value of the right to a jury trial. He told them it would take about two days to pick a jury, and that the case would take about four or five more days, after which the jury would deliberate for as long as they determined was proper. The judge asked for a show of hands of those who couldn't manage that schedule, and saw about twenty hands go up. The judge then had to conduct what is known as a "hardship" examination to see whom he should excuse. He told the panel that only certain types of excuses counted—he understood they were inconvenienced to some extent by having to serve, but that the fundamental right of trial by jury would be destroyed if everyone who found it inconvenient were to be excused. He spoke to each of the panelists who wanted to be excused, and told them that even if he excused them today they'd have to come back some other day in a month or two and go through the process all over again. When he said that, five of the hands went down. After speaking with the rest, the judge excused twelve of the panelists, and denied the hardship request of the remainder. Judge Zieff had excused one person who would probably be evicted from his apartment if he lost any days of work, and another person who had sole care of an elderly person and couldn't get anyone else to help. A number of people were excused because they had planned trips, and had paid for their tickets, for the time period when the trial would be underway One person was excused because she was a student at the local college and had classes during the time the trial would be in session.

After the hardship phase, the judge started asking questions designed to see if any of the panelists had a bias or prejudice such that it would be unfair to one side or the other to have him on the jury. The process is known as *voir dire.* The judge asked the questions he used in every case, and also invited the lawyers to submit further questions. He asked about people's feelings about driving, about drinking, whether they (or someone close to them) had been arrested for a DUI in the past, how they felt about people who worked at supermarkets. He inquired how they felt about police officers testifying (Simon had said he was going to call an officer who had investigated the scene of the accident), about whether anyone was a member of any group that endorsed or opposed the consumption of alcohol, and other questions. When he was finished, each of the lawyers got up and asked questions. Some of those questions were follow ups on what the judge had asked and some of them opened up new subjects. The judge had limited each side to twenty minutes for their portion of the *voir dire*. At one point Simon asked the panels what sort of bumper stickers they had, trying to get a sense of their politics and background. Kramer objected to the question, and the judge sustained the objection. Kramer then had to ask a different question.

After both lawyers completed their *voir dire*, they conferred privately with Judge Zieff. They each had some panelists they thought had to be excused by the judge "for cause." This means it was clear that the panelist could not be fair to one side or the other. The judge excused one panelist who said he hated cops and would never believe anything they said. He excused another who had five arrests for DUI and said that he thought laws about "drunk driving" were idiotic and he would never find against someone accused of DUI. He also excluded for cause one panelist who had said that she knew Pitt very well and would not be able to be fair to Johnson.

There was one man who was a retained investigator for insurance companies. He said that while he thought he could be fair to each side, he knew that people like Johnson were usually at fault, usually had insurance, and for that reason he would not hesitate in making a very large award in favor of the plaintiffs. The judge excused him for cause, as well. The judge refused to excuse anyone else. All had said they thought they could be fair and impartial to each side.

After the court had excused panelists for cause, each side was entitled to exercise their "preemptory challenges." Under California law, each lawyer can excuse up to six people from the panel, for any or no reason at all, but simply because the lawyer thinks they will not be good for his or her side. (Actually, there *are* some reasons that cannot be used to excuse a juror, such as those based on race, etc.).

The lawyers took turns. First Simon said, "I ask the court to thank and excuse juror number 2," and then Kramer rose and said, "I ask the court to thank and excuse juror number 10." Before he'd used all his challenges, Simon passed, indicating he was satisfied with the first twelve remaining panelists as a jury. But Kramer bumped another off, and Simon used another challenge to excuse one of the panelists. Both Kramer and Simon were looking to exclude jurors who might be problems for their side, and trying to keep jurors whom they thought would sympathize with them. Exercising these preemptory challenges is not a science; much relies on a visceral sense of the jurors. Sometimes it's just a question of a reaction to body language.

After Simon and Kramer both passed, the first twelve jurors remaining were sworn in as the jury. In the same way, two additional people were selected as alternates, in case anything happened to one of the jurors during the trial. The alternates would hear everything the jury did, and would be ready to take one of the first twelve chairs if one of the original twelve went missing for any reason.

It took almost two days to pick the jury. By the time it was all over, about ten people were left in the room, aside from the jury of twelve and the three alternates. They were thanked, and excused. They had in effect completed their jury service for the year.

Opening Statements

At the invitation of the Court (the judge is "the Court" when in session), Simon rose to give his opening statement to the jury. He was not allowed to argue as such at this stage. He was giving the jury a road map of the case, what he thought the evidence would be in the case. He had practiced, and needed no notes. He talked about his clients. He told a story. He led the jury through the night in question—the last night on earth for Hollings and one during which things would change forever for Pitt. He described Johnson's drunken evening in the bar. He told the jury that the bartender would testify, and would tell them exactly what Johnson had done. He described what the other witnesses would say, and ended up by telling them that, at the end of the case, he'd ask them for a verdict— enough to compensate Pitt for a lifetime of pain and injury and therapy, and to punish Johnson for the vicious, evil act of drinking and driving and killing. He sat down.

Kramer had practiced her opening as well. She had a fairly good idea of what Simon would say, and she was right. She stood and said nothing for ten seconds and just looked at each juror. The first words out her mouth were, "It ain't necessarily so." She told the jury that just because some lawyer gets up and says something doesn't mean it's true. She talked about a horrible accident—she wasn't going to make light of it. It was a disaster, a horrible tragedy. But that's not what this case was about. The issue for the jury was simple: did Johnson really cause the accident? Accidents happen. At night, people can't see as far they can during the day. The fact that an accident happens and one of the drivers has been drinking doesn't mean the drinking driver caused the accident. In this case, Kramer stated, the evidence would show that it was Pitt who drove through a red light, right in front of Johnson. He never had a chance to stop, drunk or sober. As Kramer pointed out, if the jury didn't find that Johnson actually caused the accident, they simply could not return a verdict for the plaintiffs.

Plaintiff's Evidence

Next, Simon started calling witness to the stand, and asking them questions. He started with Pitt, who told a vivid story about that night, and established—as least as far as Pitt was concerned—that it was Johnson who drove through a red light. Kramer cross examined each witness, and without actually making them out to be outright liars, undermined their credibility by showing the events were a long time ago, and they didn't recall too well what happened; for example, that Pitt was unconscious right after the accident. Also, Kramer had the deposition transcript Pitt had made some time back. When he talked about the events in court Kramer often was able to point out that he didn't quite say the same thing two years earlier when he had his deposition. Pitt testified for a whole day. Other witnesses testified for shorter periods. In each case, Simon went first (they are *his* witnesses after all) asking questions "on direct." Then

Kramer cross examined. Next Simon could ask questions on re-direct, as long as they had something to do with cross examination; and sometimes Kramer would re-cross (as long as the question was within the scope of the re-direct, and so on).

When one lawyer is asking questions, the other lawyer may object. When the bartender started answering questions too quickly, Kramer's objection and the answer overlapped, and the judge had to ask everyone to slow down and not talk on top of each other. Everything everyone said was being taken down by a court reporter, Judge Zieff noted, and the reporter could take down only one person's words at a time. Also, when witnesses answered questions too quickly they made it hard for the other lawyer to object. This was something the judge had to go through often, generally for each witness, because the question and answer format made it seem just like an informal conversation, and indeed the lawyers tried to encourage this feeling in the witnesses so they would loosen up and answer questions fully. As the judge pointed out, however, this was not a conversation, but a formal examination.

There are many different kinds of objections to questions. Generally the point of an objection is to prevent inadmissible evidence from coming before the jury. Inadmissible evidence usually is evidence that simply isn't very reliable. For example, if Pitt testified that he heard from a friend that Ervin Johnson used to get drunk every night, it wouldn't be fair to Johnson—people shouldn't win or lose cases based on rumors. Test results can't be introduced until the judge has a sense of how the test was conducted, that the test has some validity, and that the person conducting the test was competent. Documents can't come in before the jury unless the judge thinks that the documents are probably accurate copies, or in some other way are in fact what they purport to be. If these sorts of foundations haven't been shown, the other lawyer objects. If the objection is good, the judge *sustains* the objection and the witness cannot answer the question. If the objection is not good, the judge *overrules* the objection, and the witness is allowed to answer. If the answer comes out too fast before the judge can rule, and the objection actually is a good one, the judge will *strike* the answer and instruct the jury that it may not consider the answer at all.

Here are a few examples of typical objections. At one point while Pitt's doctor was testifying (a witnesses called by Don Simon), Simon asked the doctor, "It's true, isn't it, that all the injuries you observed were consistent with a car accident in which the other vehicle came straight into the side door of the car Pitt was in?" Kramer objected that the questions was *leading*, that is, that it led the witness to answer the way the questioner wanted, that the question itself signaled to the witness what to say. One cannot lead one's own witnesses—although it's perfectly alright when cross examining someone *else's* witness. Kramer could lead this doctor, but not Simon, because Simon called the witness in the first place.

When Kramer was cross examining the bartender, she asked, "Isn't it true that you told all your friends Ervin Johnson knew how to drink responsibly, and you never saw him drunk?" Simon did not object that the question was leading. Of course it was, but it was Kramer who was cross examining one of Simon's witnesses, so that was alright. Instead, Simon rose to his feet and objected that the question called for *hearsay*, that is, the answer would contain statements made outside the courtroom, in this case statements the bartender made some months before. The judge sustained the objection even though the person who had made those "out of court" statements was the bartender who at that moment was right in the courtroom. It didn't matter. Kramer's question called for a report on what the witness had said outside the courtroom, and that's (usually) hearsay.

Lawyers also may object to the introduction of documents, animations, and other "things" the jury might get to see. Sometimes the evidence is misleading, or there's no basis to think it's authentic, or no one has yet testified what the thing is. Sometimes the evidence is cumulative—it's just more evidence of the same point, over and over again. The judge will stop the introduction of such material and wasting everyone's time, even if one of the lawyers wants to try to make the same point over and over again.

In each case, the judge usually rules right away on objections. Sometimes he will ask the lawyers to come over to the bench. There, they will have a brief conference outside the hearing of the jury and the witness, where the lawyers can explain why they are trying to get the evidence in or why it should not be let in. These brief conferences at the side of the bench are called *sidebar conferences.*

Of course, when a judge overrules an objection, admits test results, or otherwise allows evidence to be presented to the jury, he is saying nothing about how *powerful* or *convincing* the evidence is. Very weak evidence can come in before a jury. Evidence entirely contradicted by other evidence came come in. The judge does not tell the jury what he or she thinks about the strength of the evidence (unlike in England, when in many cases judges do make such comments). Juries are entitled to weigh evidence, and otherwise give it the weight—a little, a lot, none—they think it deserves. That's their job. It doesn't matter if the evidence is that of an expert or a percipient witness, a police officer, shop owner or pilot. It's entirely up to the jury. They listen to the cross examination, they look at the way the person testifies, and a host of other factors. Based on their common sense and experience, they decide what to do with the testimony they hear.

Motion for Directed Verdict

After Simon presented all his evidence, all his witnesses were cross examined, and he introduced (or tried to introduce!) all his documents and other things he wished the jury to consider, he rested his case. That means he was finished, except for a rebuttal to any evidence the defense might put on.

At that point, at Kramer's request, the jury was asked to step out of the courtroom. Out of the hearing of the jury, Karin Kramer asked the judge to direct the verdict for her side. This was a motion for a "directed verdict," essentially, to take the case away from the jury and have the judge decide there was not enough evidence for any reasonable jury to reach a verdict for Pitt and Hollings.

The judge heard Kramer's motion for a directed verdict, and Simon's opposition to it, outside the hearing of the jury. The judge did this for a couple of reasons. First, nothing said about the motion is helpful for the jury; there's no new evidence introduced. Second, and more importantly, the jury might be swayed by the judge's ruling, and not understand that when a judge rules there is enough evidence to deny a directed verdict for one side, it doesn't mean the *other* side should win the trial. For the same reason, judges sometimes have hearings on what sort of evidence can come in outside the hearing of the jury: there may be enough of a foundation to allow the evidence to come in, but that doesn't mean the jury has to believe it, and no one wants a jury to think that a judge's positive ruling on admissibility necessarily means the evidence is important or credible.

In her motion for a directed verdict, Kramer argued that even if the jury believed everything they'd heard, no reasonable jury could possibly find for the plaintiffs. She argued that the expert whom Simon had put on had admitted that he never verified the data on which his opinion was based (his opinion that Johnson caused the crash), and that other than expert testimony, the plaintiffs had absolutely nothing on which to base their argument that Johnson was at fault.

Simon replied that experts don't have to verify all the data on which they rely. They can base their conclusions on anything that experts usually use. This data came from the National Highway Safety Commission and was the sort of data that experts always trust. Simon argued he didn't need expert testimony: Pitt had testified that the light for him and Hollings had been green, and that Johnson had come through a red light. If the jury believed that, Johnson would lose the case. Judge Zieff agreed, and denied the motion for a directed verdict. The jury was asked to come back into the courtroom.

Defendant's Evidence

Kramer then called her witnesses. She called experts, a witness called Bob Slader who said he thought the light had favored Johnson, and finally Johnson. Attorney Simon cross examined all the witnesses, and generally things proceeded as when Simon had been putting on his case. Kramer then rested, having finished putting on the evidence she wanted.

Rebuttal

Simon then had the opportunity call witnesses in rebuttal. Judge Zieff would allow these witnesses to testify only to rebut material offered by Kramer during her defense case; the judge would not allow this to be an opportunity for Simon to add to his case. The rebuttal witness was a friend of Bob Slader, who said that Slader and friend Johnson had known each other since kindergarten, were members of the same private club, and seemed to be very friendly indeed. Simon used this to cast doubt on the reliability of Slader's testimony.

Jury Instructions

A day or so into the trial, Judge Zieff had told the lawyers he wanted proposed jury instructions about three days before the contemplated end of the trial. (Well prepared lawyers have their proposed instructions ready to go the first day of trial.) Both sides looked up the standard jury instructions in books published by the Judicial Council, and by and large they each proposed the same instructions. Those instructions were about the burden of proof, what "negligence" means, what plaintiffs have to establish to win their case, how to consider witnesses' testimony, what evidence is, how to think about expert testimony, the difference between direct and circumstantial evidence, how to fill out the verdict form, and variety of other legal issues to allow the jury to understand what it would mean to return a verdict in favor of one party or the other.

But the lawyers did get into one dispute over jury instructions. Simon had found an old California appellate case which suggested it was fairly easy to prove "gross recklessness." There was language in the case that suggested it was anything other than ordinary negligence. Simon liked this language, because it would make it easier for the jury to find Johnson acted with gross recklessness which in turn would make punitive damages more likely. But Kramer objected. She said the case was out of date, and that more recent cases made it plain that the definition was in fact as stated in the Judicial Council standard instructions: it required the jury to find "callous disregard for the rights or lives" of others. Judge Zieff agreed with her, and used the instruction she proposed.

With all the evidence in, Judge Zieff read the jury instructions to the jury. It took about twenty-five minutes, and was a fairly densely packed presentation. Judge Zieff reassured the jury that they would have a copy of the instructions with them while they deliberated, and they could refer to them at any time.

Closing Arguments

After Judge Zieff finished his instructions, Don Simon stood and presented his closing argument. This time, he did indeed argue. He sought to demolish Kramer's positions. He cast Johnson in a terrible light. He asked the jury to think about Pitt, missing an arm for the rest of his life. He argued that his witnesses, and especially his experts, had presented convincing testimony. He said that Johnson's testimony was simply not credible, and asked the jury to disregard it. He showed parts of the animation again, in slow motion, displaying in excruciating detail how the truck had plowed into Hollings' car, killing her and disfiguring Pitt. He lined up ten bottles of beer on a table in the courtroom. "Those bottles did not kill Hollings," he said. "That man did," pointing to Johnson. "Make him responsible. Do the right thing." And Simon sat down.

Kramer rose, and addressed the jury in her closing argument. This is not a case about sympathy, passion or prejudice, she said. She quoted one of the jury instructions that barred the jury from basing their verdict on any of those factors. "The judge told you that," she said, "and you promised at the beginning of this trial to follow the law as the judge gives it to you. That's your sworn duty." Kramer undermined Simon's expert; she said he was good man, an intelligent man, but his opinion was worth no more than the data he relied on. And no one had come into court to verify the accuracy of that data. She said she understood how much the jury would want to give the plaintiffs a verdict, but that the justice system was just that, a justice system, where plaintiffs had actually to prove the defendant had caused the damage he was accused of causing.

Simon rose one last time, for rebuttal argument. He attacked Kramer's expert, defended Pitt and Simon's expert, and said that only *in*justice would be served if Johnson walked out of that courtroom not owing one dime to the family of the girl he'd killed and the boy he'd maimed.

He sat, finished. He was exhausted. Kramer was exhausted, but both of them sat tight-lipped as the judge had the bailiff charged under oath to take care of the jury, take them to the deliberations room, and make sure than no person except by order of the court had contact with them. The twelve jurors took all their personal belongings and notebooks, and followed the bailiff into the adjoining jury room.

Judge Zieff looked to the remaining alternates, and told them to either stick around or provide contact information where they could be reached to come to the courtroom within twenty minutes of being summoned. He reminded them they could not discuss the case with anyone, even each other, unless and until they were put on the jury. "If I do that," Judge Zieff said, "I'll instruct the jury that it must start deliberations all over again, from scratch, from the top, so you won't miss anything Any verdict with you on the jury will be the result of full and complete deliberations among all then sitting jurors."

The alternates left, one to go home fifteen minutes away, the other two to read, up in the jury assembly room. The lawyers left phone numbers with the clerk. Judge Zieff went back into chambers, took off his black robes, made himself a cup of tea, and looked out the window. After a few deep breaths, he pulled out a stack of motion papers from another case that needed to be decided by the next day, and started re-reading.

Jury Deliberations

Inside the jury room, the jurors introduced themselves and chatted a bit about the case. They had been told to pick a foreperson (or "presiding juror"), and they did that, choosing a middle school English teacher who seemed able to gently, if firmly, conduct discussions. They went around the room, everyone giving his or her initial impression about witnesses, the case, and parts of the evidence. Some were impressed by the animation, others hated it. They spoke in favor of different witnesses, and for a while chatted about how the lawyers dressed before the foreperson suggested they talk about the case. Over the space of two days they talked, sometimes on point and sometimes not. Often one or more jurors thought the majority was way off on a tangent, and vice versa. One juror kept talking about her own experiences drinking and driving, despite the other jurors' reminders that it had nothing to do with this case.

In the middle of the second day of deliberations, the jurors got into an argument about what one of the experts had said. Their notes on the testimony seemed to suggest two different points. The foreperson sent a note to the judge, asking for the testimony to be read back, but it wasn't clear from the note exactly what the jurors wanted to hear. Judge Zieff called the lawyers in—that took thirty minutes—and discussed it with them. The three agreed on a section of direct testimony and section of cross examination that seemed to address the jurors' concern, and then the three huddled with the court reporter to find that part of the trial in trial transcript. This took another thirty minutes. In the meantime, the jury was waiting but kept talking about other parts of the case. Finally, about an hour and a half after the jury asked for the read back, the court reporter was sent into the jury room to read the testimony. No one was allowed to talk to him while he did that, not to ask for any other sections to be read, and the jury was instructed not to deliberate while the court reporter completed his read back.

Later, the jurors got into another argument, this time about the jury instruction that dealt with the definition of "negligence." Two jurors said they still didn't understand it. A note was sent out to the judge, asking for another definition. The judge again consulted with the lawyers. Simon came up with another definition, something to the effect that negligence meant "doing something without thinking about it." Karin Kramer strongly disagreed. She said that any verdict based on such a definition simply would be reversed on appeal. Finally the judge realized he couldn't be of much help to the jury. The courts of appeal opinions, and approved jury instructions, were plain about the definition to be provided to the jury. He wrote the jury back a note, saying he was unable to provide a different definition.

Verdict

The jury voted twice in the first day and a half of deliberation. Almost two full days after closing argument, the jury took a third vote. It was the same as the second vote that they had taken a few hours earlier, 10-2 for the plaintiffs. The majority had tried to convince the two hold outs, but those two were firmly convinced that there was not enough evidence that Johnson had really caused the accident. But since more than ¾ of the civil jury agreed, they had enough for a verdict and started filling out the verdict form. First, they indicated that the verdict was for the plaintiff. They discussed compensatory damages: money to compensate for pain and suffering, lost wages, medical bills, other out of pocket expenses, and the like, bills incurred to date and what were reasonably foreseeable expenses into the future. They agreed on a sum of $1,000,000 for Hollings and $2,000,000 for Pitt since he would have medical expenses for the rest of his life. It was ironic that the death was, in a sense, worth less than the life left.

When the verdict was filled out, the presiding juror signed and dated it, and knocked on the door of the jury room. The bailiff opened it, and the presiding juror said they had a verdict. The bailiff notified the judge's clerk, who then called the judge.

The lawyers were summoned: the jury had a verdict. The jury waited in their room, waiting to be called into the courtroom. Now that the case was over, they thought, there was very little to say to each other. Some read a newspaper, others made notes to themselves about the experience. Time went by. The jury looked at each other, thinking about the extraordinary past two weeks.

The attorneys and clients arrived in the courtroom. The judge took the bench, and the bailiff was asked to bring the jurors in. As always, all stood while the jury entered or left the courtroom, as a sign of respect for their central role in the justice system. None of the jurors looked at the lawyers. They sat in their seats.

The judge asked, "Have you elected a foreperson?" Number seven raised her hand. The judge asked her, "Has the jury reached a verdict?" "Yes," she replied. "Please pass the verdict form to the bailiff," the judge instructed.

The bailiff took the folded over piece of paper and gave it to Judge Zieff, who kept a poker face as he read over the form to make sure it was filled out correctly, signed and dated by the foreperson. It was. He gave it to the bailiff who handed it to the clerk of the court. "The clerk will read the verdict," Judge Zieff announced.

"In the matter of Hollings and Pitt versus Johnson, Number 4637789 in the Superior Court of the State of California, City and County of San Francisco, we the jury find in favor of the plaintiffs Pitt and Hollings and against Johnson, in the amount of one million dollars for Hollings and two millions dollars for Pitt. Signed, dated, by the Foreperson." The clerk also read out some the special findings, including one in which the jury agreed that Johnson had acted with gross recklessness.

Simon flushed, breathed out a sigh of relief. It was as he hoped. It wasn't over, not by a long shot, but he had his verdict. Kramer was still. She thought this might be coming, and she was ready for the verdict. But that didn't make it any easier to handle. She—and Simon, of course—had worked on this case for years, and it all came down to these twelve people they had never met before and would never meet again, looking at all the evidence at once, talking to each other, deciding the case for millions of dollars, and then leaving forever, to go back to their own lives....

The judge was talking. He thanked the jury and told them they still had one more piece of business. The judge explained that under law he was unable to discuss with them, until now, the issue of punitive damages. But now that they had found in favor of the plaintiffs on compensatory damages and that Johnson had acted recklessly, the plaintiffs were entitled to put on a case for punitive damages, damages designed to punish Johnson for his acts, and to deter others from doing the same thing in the future. That would take another half day.

The next day, Simon put on evidence of how much Johnson was worth: what his assets were, how much he made. He argued that most of it should be turned over to the plaintiffs as punishment. Kramer argued that while the jury had found Johnson liable for recklessness, it wasn't as bad as, say, an intentional act—intentionally ramming his truck into the car owned by Hollings. It had in fact been an accident; he never had meant to hurt anyone. So they shouldn't punish him by stripping him of everything he owned, and in any event the jury had already ensured that the plaintiffs would be compensated; anything else would just be a windfall. Both lawyers knew that a lot depended on just how angry the jurors were about Johnson's acts. There was another shorter closing argument from both sides. Johnson didn't have many assets anyway and the jury decided to award half of them to Pitt and Hollings in punitive damages. The case—in the trial court—was over. Almost.

Kramer made post trial motions to reduce the verdict, to set aside the verdict and have a new trial. Those motions took two months to prepare and argue. Judge Zieff denied the motions, and entered judgment on the verdict—which means the verdict of the jury became the final judgment of the court.

Now the case over; at least, in the Superior Court.

Appeal to the Court of Appeal

Kramer talked to her client about an appeal. It would cost money, money that Johnson really did not have. (In our story, of course, the costs of litigation were paid by the insurance company.) But on the other hand perhaps the case might settle on appeal, or if the case were actually reversed, Simon might agree to a substantial reduction in the verdict instead of having to litigate the case all over again. Johnson asked what the odds were of success on appeal. Kramer told him frankly that most judgments are affirmed, but that in this case they had one potentially good argument. The plaintiff's accident reconstruction expert had provided inaccurate data to the visual artist who designed the animation of the accident. The pitch to the court of appeal would be that because the animation was a powerful kind of argument—a "pretend" visualization of the accident, Kramer put it—that it must have profoundly affected the verdict. Kramer estimated the odds of reversal around 20%. At this point Johnson was in jail for the next eleven years, and he told her to go ahead. He had little to lose.

Kramer filed a notice of appeal in the Superior Court. One page. It said simply that Johnson appealed the judgment. At that point the case was out of the hands of Judge Zieff, and in the court of appeal—specifically, the First District Court of Appeal in San Francisco. Like the other courts of appeal, the First District takes appeals from the final judgments in the superior courts. It also has the authority to issue writs to the superior courts to do or not do certain things, even if a final judgment has not been entered. For example, in our case Simon had been very concerned that Judge Zieff might order Pitt to disclose communications between Pitt and Simon, his lawyer. If Judge Zieff had done this, the damage to the attorney client communication privilege (not to reveal this sort of communications) would have been irreparable, and Simon would have sought a writ from the Court of Appeal before complying. The Court of Appeal very, very rarely steps in this way, but they might have for this sort of emergency situation. It's entirely up to the Court of Appeal whether it issues these sorts of writs or not.

It is *not* up to the appellate court to decide whether to take an appeal or not. It must hear it. So when Kramer filed her notice of appeal, she knew that, one way or the other, she would get a ruling from the Court of Appeal.

The next half year was occupied with preparing the formal transcript of the trial, designating which parts of the trial, which evidence and which rulings, which court orders, and so on both lawyers wanted the Court of Appeal to see. This is calling preparing the *record on appeal*. Finally, the lawyers were able to tell the court of appeal that the record was ready, and the clerk of the court of appeal issued an order setting forth the briefing schedule. Kramer, as the lawyer appealing—the appellant— would get the first shot, the opening brief. Simon would file an opposition brief. After that, Kramer would file a reply brief.

Some months afterwards, the Court of Appeal issued an order setting the case down for oral argument. This was, by now, about four years after the accident.

By the date of the oral argument before the Court of Appeal, the three judge panel had already looked at the case and made a preliminary decision on how to handle it. One of the three justices takes responsibility for each case that comes through the court, and the justice handling this case had had her clerks research the matter, read the record on appeal, and suggest a decision. By the time the case was ready for argument, the court of appeal justices had exchanged preliminary thoughts on the matter, and were ready for argument.

Some justices on the courts of appeal think oral argument is helpful. Others do not. It has been said that while appeals cases are rarely won as a result of the oral argument, they can be lost at oral argument. Some courts of appeal have argument only if one side or the other insists.

The case was the third case to be argued that morning in the Court of Appeal. Simon and Kramer had spent the last two weeks going over every case cited in every brief and re-reading the record on appeal, trying to anticipate questions from the justices. Simon spent time doing a "moot court," which means he got some friends to play being the justices, grilling him and engaging in mock arguments. Kramer did a lot of yoga and went for ten-mile bike rides.

The case was called, and Kramer stepped up to the lectern facing the three judge panel. Before she had her first sentence out, one of the justices fired a question at her about what standard the court should use in reviewing the judgment below, the judgment in the superior court. Just as she finished answering the question, another justice asked her a question about the testimony of one of the expert witnesses, and the first justice went back to standards of review. The third justice asked her about a key footnote in one of the important cases that Simon has cited in his brief— and on it went from there. Before she knew it, Kramer saw a white light go off on the lectern, indicating five minutes left. She stopped and asked to reserve her last few minutes for her rebuttal. She wanted to have the last word after Simon finished. Her request was granted by the presiding justice, who sat in the middle of the two associate justices on the panel and controlled the courtroom proceedings.

For the first five minutes of Simon's argument, there were no questions at all, and it made him very, very nervous. For a moment he thought he was talking about the wrong case. Suddenly two of the justices started asking questions, and again before he knew it first the white, then the red, lights came on. He obediently sat down.

Kramer rose for her rebuttal, focusing on one of Simon's argument which she thought was his strongest. Simon had discussed the fact that, even if the judge below had been wrong in his ruling to admit the animation, the visual recreation of the accident, the Court of Appeal should be very hesitant to reverse the judgment. Trial courts were to be accorded a lot of deference in their evidentiary rulings, and even if the animation should not have been viewed by the jury, the Court of Appeal could not reverse unless they found the verdict would likely have been different. There was so much evidence of Johnson's liability, other than the animation, that Johnson would have lost anyway, Simon argued. Kramer vigorously disputed this. She said that the animation was the single key focus of the entire trial. It had been so important that Simon had actually played it again and again, the final time in his closing argument. It had inflamed and impassioned the jury, and even if they would have found against her client Johnson, they never would have awarded so much money to the plaintiffs.

Four minutes later the red light went off at her lectern, indicating time was up. Lawyers never may go past their time unless invited to do so by a justice. Kramer stopped and sat down.

"Case submitted," said the presiding justice, and turned to the next case. Simon and Kramer walked out of the courtroom, shook hands, and went to their offices to work on their other cases. Neither would hear anything from the Court of Appeal for months. Kramer had the sense that things had not gone well, and that Simon was unlikely to want to settle the case for anything her client actually could afford. She called Simon up to talk about settlement, but he politely suggested they wait for the ruling from the Court of Appeal.

Three months later the Court of Appeal issued a written opinion affirming the judgment in the Superior Court.

Filing Certiorari Petition to the Supreme Court

Kramer went back to speak to her client, Ervin Johnson, about trying to get the California Supreme Court to take the case, to try to get the Court of Appeal reversed.   Johnson asked about the odds of success. Kramer explained that the Supreme Court takes cases rarely, and only when there is something important about the case, important not just to the parties in the case, but to others as well. Examples were if the Court of Appeal had announced a rule of law in conflict with other courts, if there were some novel issue of law, and so on. Kramer was frank with her client: although the Court of Appeal may have made an error in this particular case, that was not enough to get the Supreme Court to grant certiorari and take the case. The "petition for cert" very likely would be denied. Johnson told her to forget it, thanked her for all her work, and left the meeting room.

Executing on the Judgment

About two months after the Court of Appeal issued its decision, a formal paper issued from that court back to the Superior Court, transferring the entire case back to the trial court. At that point, Simon could start executing on the judgment, which means taking steps to get the money the jury had awarded. Simon had a variety of options. He could demand to take a statement under oath of all of Johnson's assets in order to locate them. He could send notices to banks and tell them to take money from Johnson's accounts and transfer it to him, for the plaintiffs. Simon could have Johnson's properties sold to raise the money needed to pay the judgment.

Because Johnson had been covered by insurance, the insurance company paid up the maximum of the policy coverage, which in this case was $250,000. For the rest of the millions Simon had won, Simon had to seize Johnson's assets such as his savings and back accounts. Johnson was married, and almost all his assets were owned jointly by himself and his wife. When the assets were seized, Johnson's wife, too, was devastated.

But Johnson and his wife didn't have the millions of dollars the jury had awarded. After four months of investigation, Simon had done all he could to find Johnson's assets. He took a third of the recovery for himself (he was entitled to this under his contingency agreement), and sent the rest to Hollings' family and to Pitt.

It was time for all of them to turn to other things.

Chapter 13: A Story about a Criminal Case

This chapter tells the story of the companion criminal case. Here the People of the State of California charged Johnson with a crime-- driving while under the influence of alcohol, and second degree murder. Johnson was represented in this case by the Office of the Public Defender. He was not represented by Karin Kramer, who as a civil litigation lawyer had little experience in criminal law procedures. The Public Defender uses public funds to make sure that all people accused of a crime are represented by a lawyer, even if they cannot afford it.

The People, or the prosecution, is represented by the county's District Attorney's office. The District Attorney and the Public Defender are public officials and they are responsible for the hiring of attorneys to staff their offices. The lawyers actually involved in this case we will simply refer to as the assistant district attorney, or "DA" and the assistant public defender, or "PD." In the state system, crimes are investigated by the police, investigators for the District Attorney, the California Highway Patrol, and other agencies.

The DA and her assistant district attorneys, and investigators, together with the Highway Patrol and other police, are from the executive branch. They must enforce the laws made by the legislative branch. They bring in cases to be decided by the judicial branch.

The Public Defender is not really a part of any of the three branches of government at all, although he and the lawyers he hires to be assistant public defenders are paid with public funds. In San Francisco (as opposed to other places) the Public Defender does not answer to the mayor, the governor, or any other person in the executive branch. Instead, he runs for office on his own, and can be replaced by the voting public. In San Francisco, the Public Defender does have to have his budget approved by the mayor (executive branch) and the city council (legislative branch). In other counties, the Public Defender is hired by the county administration. Like all lawyers, the public defenders and district attorneys are responsible to the courts, and must follow the orders of the judges.

Like all lawyers, they must comply with a series of rules called the Rules of Professional Responsibility. Those Rules are enforced by an organization called the State Bar—the association of lawyers in the state. All lawyers must belong to the State Bar, and must take a test to become a member. In most states, only people who have graduated from a law school are allowed to take that test. The State Bar can investigate lawyers who fail to adhere to the Rules of Professional Conduct, and can "disbar" those lawyers. If disbarred, a person may not practice law. Indeed, it is a *crime* to practice law if one is not a member of the Bar. (By the way, judges are not allowed to be members of the Bar—they have to resign if they are appointed. That means that judges can't give legal advice or otherwise practice law.)

In our story the crime is charged by the DA, who is a state official, and the case is handled in the state courts, i.e. the superior court. If the case had involved a federal crime, then it would have been investigated by federal authorities such as the FBI, the Secret Service, the Bureau of Alcohol Tobacco and Firearms (ATF), U.S. Customs, and so on. The case then would have been prosecuted by federal prosecutors (the U.S. Attorney's Office) and been heard before a federal judge, i.e., the local U.S. District Court. As suggested earlier in this book, federal crimes involve some federal interest, such as crimes that take place in more than one state, on federal property, or have to do with matters such as the Securities and Exchange Commission (which regulates the national stock markets), international trade and so on, for which Congress has passed criminal laws.

In our scenario, a police officer found Johnson on the scene of the accident, and determined that an accident had occurred and that Johnson appeared to be under the influence of alcohol (DUI). The officer decided this after closely observing Johnson, seeing his performance on so-called 'field sobriety checks,' and having him take a breath test which showed more than the legal limit of alcohol in his blood. Johnson was arrested on the spot and taken first to the hospital, where he was treated for injuries sustained in the accident. There, the police had a blood sample taken from him. This too showed a high level of blood alcohol.

Johnson was taken, in custody, to court after being treated at the hospital. There the Public Defender's Office (PD) was appointed to represent him. The district attorney's office prepared a document that listed the charges against Johnson. This is the "complaint," and it was provided to the PD. It included felony charges of second degree murder. The PD asked for Johnson to be released on his own recognizance ("OR"), that is, just on his promise to return for his next court dates. Johnson had prior convictions for DUI some years in the past, but never had missed a court date. No bench warrant—a warrant for arrest issued by a judge when the defendant fails to show up for a hearing—ever had been issued for his arrest. On the other hand, the judge was concerned about his possible danger to the community if he were released. Also, Johnson was charged with a very serious felony, and stood to lose a lot if he were convicted. The judge considered all these factors as he decided whether or not to release the defendant on his OR. He decided not to release Johnson on his own recognizance, and instead decided to set bail at $400,000. (Actually, in a murder case the judge might well not have allowed Johnson out on bail at all, but we depart from this to illustrate the bail system.)

Setting bail at $400,000 means that Johnson could get released if he did one of two things. Johnson could get $400,000 in cash, or sign over property to the court worth that. His second option was to go to a bail bond company and get them to post the $400,000. This probably would cost Johnson ten percent ($40,000) as a nonrefundable cost or 'premium.' At the end of the case, if he posted the entire $400,000 himself, he'd get the money back. If he had to get a bail bondsman to post the money, he would not get back his $40,000 premium. Johnson didn't have $400,000, and he didn't have $40,000 in cash for the bond, so he signed over his house, with an appraised value of over $400,000. If he failed to make any court date or his bail were revoked for any reason, he would lose the house. But having posted bail, he was freed from county jail pending his trial.

Infractions vs. Misdemeanors vs. Felonies

If the DUI had not been so serious, it is possible that Johnson could have been charged with a misdemeanor DUI instead of the felony. A misdemeanor is punishable by up to a year in the county jail. Felonies are more serious, and are punishable by years in the state prison. Less serious than misdemeanors are infractions, which are punishable only by fines and no jail time.

Probable Cause and the Role of the Grand Jury

Both the state and federal systems use grand juries in their investigations. "Grand" juries are called this to distinguish them from "petit" (or small) juries—the juries of 12 used to determine the verdict in most cases. Grand juries are, as the name suggests, much larger bodies, consisting of about 30 people. Grand juries are managed by prosecutors, and have the power both to compel witnesses to come and give testimony under oath as they investigate a crime, and to indict (pronounced "indite"), which means to charge someone with a crime. The grand jury indicts only if there is "probable cause" to believe a crime has been committed and that the defendant did it. In the federal system almost all crimes are indicted by the grand jury. In the California state system, only a handful of serious crimes are indicted. Instead of an indictment which lists the charges, most state criminal cases commence with a paper called a complaint, listing the charges. The complaint is issued in the state system by the DA's office.

When grand juries indict people for felonies, they have made a finding of "probable cause." This is a finding that there is sufficient evidence or proof that a crime has been committed and that the defendant has committed it. But otherwise, people are charged without that finding, so the law has procedures to make sure no one is held without such a finding. Judges, as independent neutral reviewers, must determine whether there is probable cause, and if not, the person cannot be held and the case must be dismissed. In misdemeanors, at the time the person is first brought to court, his lawyer can ask the judge to make a determination, right then and there, that there is no probable cause. Usually the judge looks over the police report, to see if, making inferences in favor of the People, every element of the crime is supported by something in the police report. If not, the case is dismissed.

For felonies, the procedures are more complicated. Judges actually have hearings devoted to probable cause. Indeed, in San Francisco and many other counties, as well as in other states, there are judges who do nothing except conduct probable cause hearings. These are called "preliminary hearings" or "prelims" for short. Now, as a matter of practice, when the lawyers get together for the hearing, they also talk about plea bargains. Many cases are actually "disposed of" on the day of the hearing, which means some deal is worked out and the defendant pleads to some charge in exchange for an agreed-upon sentence. This is a plea bargain. Otherwise the preliminary hearing goes forward, which is very much like a short version of the trial. Sometimes a police officer simply recites the results of his investigation; sometimes the witnesses themselves come and testify. In the end, the judge does the same thing as if it were a misdemeanor case. She decides if there is probable cause, and if so, the defendant is "held to answer" or "bound over for trial" which means there's enough to set the case for a jury trial. Otherwise, the case is either tossed out—the changes are dismissed—or the judge reduces the charges to what they should be, based on the evidence. For example, in our scenario, if Johnson had been charged with first degree murder based on his role in the death of Hollings, the judge at the preliminary hearing might have reduced the charges to vehicular manslaughter, or some other charge, if the judge didn't think the People had enough evidence of an element of first degree murder (such as premeditation).

In our case there was a preliminary hearing. The DA and the PD talked about settling the case, but couldn't agree on what the sentence should be. So the DA went ahead and put on his case. He called a police officer and the bartender to testify. The officer was allowed to testify about a conversation she'd had with Pitt who was still in the hospital at the time. All told the hearing took half a day, and at the end the judge found there was enough evidence for probable cause, and held Johnson to answer. Johnson had a 'speedy trial' right to have the case set for trial in about a month, but his lawyer wanted more time to prepare, so she "waived time" and agreed that it would be set down in four months.

Motion to Suppress

Before the case went to a jury trial, however, the PD wanted to set a motion to suppress. He knew that the police had seized a few things, and the PD wanted them excluded from evidence at the upcoming trial. First, the police had seized blood from Johnson after he was arrested: they had taken him to the hospital after the arrest and there a sample of his blood had been taken. The test results on the blood were grim: twice the legal limit. If the blood were suppressed, the evidence of the test would be suppressed as well. The jury never would hear about the blood test results. The police also had searched Johnson's car after the accident: the car had been towed, and a search conducted at the towing parking lot. The search revealed two empty bottles of beer. The PD wanted those bottles suppressed, as well. No judge had issued a search warrant for the blood sample, or for the search of the car. So the burden would be on the DA, the People, to show that the searches had been, even without a warrant, reasonable.

Often the motion to suppress actually is handled at the same time as the preliminary hearing. For our purposes and to keep the issues distinct, we'll assume it's a separate hearing.

The motion to suppress was heard by a judge in the criminal division of the Superior Court about a month after the arrest. The DA called the investigating police officer as his witness. The officer described the events of the evening: the call from dispatch he'd received over his radio in his car, driving to the scene of the accident, and what he saw there. Both Johnson's truck and Hollings' car were seriously damaged, and for that reason he eventually had both towed. Inventory searches of towed cars are routinely done because the police are responsible for safeguarding the contents while in their custody. It was that search that uncovered the beer bottles. The officer described Johnson at the scene: red, watery eyes and stumbling, incoherent speech. Johnson was unable to do any of the field sobriety tests, such as walking a straight line, lifting one leg up and counting out loud, and so on. The Officer had Johnson breathe into a preliminary alcohol screening device ("PAS"), a small, portable computer which analyses breath for alcohol content. The PAS suggested Johnson was at least twice over the legal limit. For that reason, he was arrested, and transported to the hospital where the blood sample was taken. Next, the DA called as a witness the phlebotomist, a trained person who draws blood. She discussed her steps, the use of sterile needles, how the area on the arm was swabbed, how she drew the blood and put it in three sealed capsules, and so on.

For both witnesses, the PD conducted a cross examination. The PD had the police officer admit that red, watery eyes might be normal late at night and might not indicate someone was drunk; that many people, out of nervousness and so on, might fail one or more field sobriety tests; and that the PAS device hadn't been checked in a month before the evening in question. The PD also attacked the blood draw, and had the phlebotomist admit that she did about twenty of these per month, that the blood draw had been a long time ago. The PD tried to have her admit that she couldn't really recall what had happened during this particular blood draw.

After about thirty minutes the motion to suppress hearing was over. The judge, who had been taking notes, read his ruling out loud. He found that the officer had acted reasonably in having the car towed, and that there was nothing wrong with the subsequent inventory search. The two beer bottles would not be suppressed. He found that there had been probable cause for the arrest of Johnson, plus that the blood draw was reasonable, valid in the sense that it had been done by a competent professional who had used standard medical procedures. Thus the seizure of Johnson and of his blood was reasonable and valid, and so the blood would not be suppressed.

The motion to suppress was denied. The People would be allowed to use the challenged evidence at trial.

Pretrial Discussions and Settlement Explorations

Just as in civil cases, the parties try to settle their criminal cases. About ten percent of the cases go to trial; the rest settle for an agreed-upon sentence, or the case is dismissed. Sometimes the lawyers simply call each other on the phone, or they might discuss the case at a pretrial conference the judge might have. For felonies, many of these settlement discussions take place just before the preliminary hearing. In federal courts the judge generally plays no role in settlements; in California state courts, the judge may be involved and often tries to help the parties reach a resolution. Defendants can plead guilty (or "no contest") in return for a sentence that the DA agrees to, or they can "plead open to the court" which means they simply plead 'no contest' or 'guilty' generally in return for a sentence indicated by the judge. The usual idea is to offer the defendant an incentive to change his plea, and so the offers usually are more favorable to the defendant before trial than what he might expect to get if he were convicted by a jury.

In our case, the DA and PD met with the judge at 8:30 A.M., the day the preliminary hearing was scheduled. The DA offered Johnson fifteen years in state prison. Johnson turned down the offer, and his PD asked the judge what the judge would sentence him to if he pled open to the court.

Pleading "open" to the judge means, in effect, making a deal directly with the judge. If asked, California judges will usually indicate what they believe to be a reasonable sentence, based on what they know then about the defendant. They look at the severity of the offense, the defendant's prior record, and other facts brought to their attention by the PD and the DA. If a defendant pleads guilty to a felony in connection with a deal with the DA, or as a result of an indicated sentence from a judge, a pre-sentence report is prepared, which details all the facts about a defendant, and about the crime, which might be useful to a judge in sentencing. Sometimes the pre-sentence report will show that the agreed-upon sentence is wrong—for example, the pre-sentence report might reveal for the first time that the defendant had been convicted many times before, or that he committed the new crime while on probation. In such a case, an indicated sentence that just put him back on probation might not be reasonable, in the judge's opinion. In such a situation, the judge informs the defendant, for example, that the judge will not impose the indicated sentence but wants to impose a harsher sentence; the defendant then has the right to withdraw his previous guilty plea, and the case proceeds just as if the defendant never had made a deal.

In our case, the judge was asked for an indicated sentence if Johnson pled open to the court. The judge indicated that, based on what he had in front of him at the moment, he didn't see he could improve on the DA's offer significantly. The DA said he'd ask for twenty years after trial; the PD shrugged that off, and the preliminary hearing took place later that morning.

Discovery

Parties exchange information in advance of the trial, and parties have "discovery" rights, as they do in civil cases. Discovery is far more limited in criminal cases, primarily because there are far fewer documents that matter to the outcome. Criminal cases also must be processed much faster than civil cases, because defendants have rights under state and federal constitutions, and under state statutory law, to have their cases heard in rapid order. These rights are sometimes known as "speedy trial" rights.

Discovery in criminal cases is governed by both (1) statutes and (2) state and federal constitutions.

Statutory Rights

Under state law, certain kinds of information have to be exchanged. Each side must provide the other with the names and addresses of witnesses they expect to call at trial. The People (the prosecutor) must make available to the defendant all evidence they intend to introduce. The parties also have to exchange any recorded statements from their witnesses, as well as any reports authored by their experts.

Defense lawyers also can ask for other things, and if they don't get them they can make a motion to have the court order the People to produce those items. For example, in our case the PD asked the DA for all records relating to the maintenance, repair and checks of the two machines used to check for alcohol in Johnson's blood.

Constitutional Rights (due process) - Exculpatory Evidence

There are some things the People must give to the defense, because the defendant's constitutional right to due process is at stake. Exculpatory evidence is evidence which might show the defendant is innocent, or which might cast some doubt on the People's version of events or on the People's witnesses. Prosecutors must turn over all exculpatory evidence. The People run criminal arrest checks on all their witnesses, and provide the results to the defense.

There are many varieties of exculpatory evidence. Obviously, the fact that a witness for the prosecution has a long criminal record might be exculpatory. Also included are police reports and information of other possible perpetrators of the crime, scientific tests that don't confirm the People's theory of the case, and so on.

Trial

The criminal case of *People v. Johnson* was set for trial on March 7, many months after the accident. The case was assigned to Judge Baldwin in the Superior Court's criminal courts, who first met with the attorneys. He made a final effort at settling the case, and then walked the parties through a checklist of issues, including how he picked juries, how evidence had to be marked (each piece is marked with a number or a letter), where to stand when asking questions of witnesses, and other guidelines. He asked how many witnesses were expected, how long the case would be, whether foreign language interpreters were needed, and if there were any motions contemplated which might have to be raised outside the presence of the jury. For example, if the defense thought that a statement had been taken from Johnson while he was in custody, but before his *Miranda* rights were read to him, the issue of whether or not the statements would be admitted had to be handled outside the hearing of the jury so that, if the court ruled that the statements were inadmissible, the jury would not be tainted by hearing about them as the motion to exclude was being argued. Other motions, too, have to be made outside the presence of the jury, such as motions based on prosecutorial misconduct, or for a judgment of acquittal. If the jury hears these motions being argued, they might be swayed one way or the other by what the lawyers or the judge say.

Judge Baldwin invited counsel to suggest questions for *voir dire*, and indicated when he wanted proposed jury instructions. Each side had a series of preliminary motions they wanted the judge to rule on, such as to exclude certain evidence, and to make sure witnesses who were not testifying were excluded from the courtroom (so they would not tailor their testimony to what others said).

Virtually all criminal trials are before juries, and almost never before the judge in a bench trial. Unless the charge is an infraction, defendants have a right to a jury trial. The burden of proof at a criminal trial is very different from the burden at a civil trial. Recall that a *preponderance* of the evidence is enough to win the civil trial, for either side. And in a civil case in California, a verdict can be returned by a jury even if only 9 people agree to it. In a criminal trial, by contrast, the People must prove every element of the case *beyond a reasonable doubt,* and all 12 jurors must agree. Here's what some judges might read to the jury panel about reasonable doubt:

> "In a criminal case, the defendant is presumed to be innocent until the contrary is proved, and in case of a reasonable doubt, he/she is entitled to a not guilty verdict. The effect of this presumption is simply to place upon the state the burden of proving the defendant guilty beyond a reasonable doubt. Until and unless this is done, the presumption of innocence prevails. Proof beyond a reasonable doubt is proof that leaves you with an abiding conviction that the charge is true. The evidence need not eliminate all possible doubt, because everything relating to human affairs is open to some possible or imaginary doubt."

Jury Selection

Judge Baldwin spent the first hour or so welcoming the panel of 80 people sent to his courtroom from the Jury Assembly Room. He told them how long the case would be, and evaluated hardship excuses, very much as he would have in a civil case. Jury selection—known as *voir dire*—then proceeded much as it would in a civil case, except there were additional questions asked of the panel to evaluate their feelings about police, the DA's office, and the criminal process generally. They were asked if they would have a problem with the reasonable doubt standard, or the presumption of innocence. There were a few jurors who said they thought the defendant must probably be guilty if he were here in court. The judge reminded them of the presumption of innocence, and asked it they could follow his instruction that they must not be biased against Johnson just because he'd been charged and brought to trial. Judge Baldwin excused those who appeared to have difficulty with the instruction. He also excused panelists who had in the past had very bad experiences with police and said they didn't think they could put those experiences behind them. A few panelists said they had zero tolerance for drinking and driving, didn't really care about the law on that subject, and indicated they'd follow their own views. They were excused. One person had been in an accident just three months earlier in which there had been allegations that the other driver had been drinking; she was excused.

During the *voir dire* that day, there were a variety of other disclosures that came up as the judge, and then the lawyers, asked their questions. It happened that some of the people worked in bars, some did not have driver's licenses at all; many of the panelists volunteered that they did not like drunk driving; none of those issues was relevant to their being excused by the Court. (No one "likes" criminal behavior, but every case in criminal court involves allegations of that behavior.) Many people had either been arrested in the past or been victims of some sort of criminal behavior, but in almost all cases they said those experiences would not affect their ability to be fair and impartial to each side.

There were some people who seemed willing to say anything to get off the jury. Although all panelists were sworn to tell the truth, Judge Baldwin had suspicions that a few were saying things that were not true. It was disturbing and depressing: these were people who would fervently wish for a jury if they ever were involved in litigation. These were people who took all the benefits of living in a free society, and enjoyed the rights guaranteed by the Constitution, but were unwilling to do much to contribute. Most of the rest of the panel, hearing these apparently made-up excuses, knew exactly what was going on. Towards the end of the day,

Judge Baldwin asked these malcontents to leave, feeling they would not perform their duties conscientiously.

When, after discussing the matter with the lawyers outside the hearing of the jury, Judge Baldwin had excused those whom he did not think could be impartial and fair, the lawyers exercised their peremptory challenges, in turn, striking the names of panelists they did not want on the jury. (In this case, each side got 15 "peremptories" or opportunities to strike a person from the panel.) The DA used up all his peremptories. After the PD passed (satisfied with the first 12 left), the DA had to accept the jury as it then was. The lawyers then exercised a further set of peremptories, and the alternates were selected. The clerk swore in the jury of 12, and then the two alternates. By that time it was the end of the day, and the judge sent the jury home, first instructing them that they could not talk to anyone, even each other, about the case, the issues and people involved in it, and to form no opinion at all about how the case should come out.

Opening Statements

The next day the DA gave her opening statement. It was brief and to the point. She briefly alluded to her burden to prove the case beyond a reasonable doubt, and told the jury she accepted the burden willingly, and that in this case they would have no doubt of Johnson's guilt. She outlined the evidence she expected to be presented, and told the jury she would be asking them for a guilty verdict at the end of the trial.

The PD rose, and gave an opening statement. He could have declined to do so, or he could have waited until the People's case was over and given his opening at the beginning of a defense case. But he wanted the jury to understand, from the very beginning, that the evidence would be contested, that it was going to be tough for the People to prove their case beyond a reasonable doubt. He told the jury that they had to keep an open mind. Even if all they heard at the beginning of the trial was the evidence as the People would like them to hear it, they had to keep an open mind and not decide the case until *all* the evidence had been heard.

People's Evidence

Many of the witnesses who would later testify at the civil case testified in this criminal case. Pitt, of course, was the key witness, at once displaying to the jury the damage done to him in the car accident, and testifying that the light had been against Johnson. The bartender testified about Johnson's drinking, and the police testified about his arrest and the taking of blood samples. They also testified on the field sobriety tests. The county coroner testified on the cause of death of Hollings, and a doctor spoke about the injuries to Pitt.

When witnesses are asked questions by the party who called them to trial, they are testifying on "direct." When they answer questions by the *other* side, they are under "cross examination." Pitt, the bartender, and the police all first were asked questions by the prosecutor "on direct."

The PD then cross examined all of those witnesses. In each, the point was not to get them to contradict themselves, or to have them admit they were lying, but rather to undermine any claim to certainty, to demonstrate to the jury that questions remained about each part of the People's case. For example, on cross examination, which the PD could conduct using leading questions, the bartender said he didn't know exactly how many beers Johnson had. The officer testified on direct about field sobriety tests. The cross examination revealed that many of them were not scientifically validated, that they required a degree of judgment on the part of the officer to evaluate, that they were not "pass/fail" tests but that different people, even when sober, performed differently on these. Then the PD went after the experts who testified about the machines used to test Johnson's breath for alcohol. One of the machines used in the field by the arresting officer was the PAS device; the other was an Intoxilizer machine used at the police station. In each case, the machines took breath samples and estimated the blood alcohol level. None of the witnesses knew the details of how the machines worked. Each machine had been tested and repaired in the past; neither one was always perfectly accurate, sometimes reading slightly high. The Intoxilizer machine was 15 years old. The PD emphasized these issues in his cross-examination.

On redirect, the DA established that both machines had passed reliability tests just before the night in question, and were operating within certain limits of accuracy.

As the officer who arrested Johnson was testifying, he blurted out something that none of the lawyers had previously known, and that was not referred to in the police report. The officer said that a few seconds after Johnson was arrested, he'd said to the officer, "Ok, ya got me, I crashed into the stupid car." The PD immediately leapt to his feet and asked for a sidebar conference, to talk about this outside the hearing of the jury.

Within a few seconds at sidebar Judge Baldwin realized the issue was not simple and would take more than a few seconds to address. He turned to the jury, gave them a twenty-minute break, and excused them from the courtroom. Then, once the jury was gone, the lawyers were able to talk about the problem on the record (with everything being said taken down by the court reporter). The PD asked for a mistrial, that is, to discharge the jury and terminate the trial. The basis for the request was that the PD had never known of this prior statement of the defendant, and it was the absolute obligation of the People to disclose any such statements long before trial. Further, the statement appeared to have been made while Johnson was in custody but before the *Miranda* warnings had been read to him, so the statements were presumptively coerced under *Miranda*, and were not admissible at the trial—but here they were, with the jury having heard the entire statement which the PD said was tantamount to a confession. Nothing except a mistrial would cure the problem—the jury could not be told now to pretend they had not heard the words.

It was a serious issue for the DA. If the judge declared a mistrial, there was some question whether Johnson could be retried; if not, the charges would have to be dismissed. The problem was one of *double jeopardy*: a defendant can be tried only once for a crime—that is a guarantee from the U.S. Constitution. There are exceptions, but if the mistrial is declared as a result of bad acts by the People, double jeopardy might bar a second bite at the apple. In such a case, the defendant would go free.

The immediate issue, however, was what the Judge would do about the statements blurted out by the officer. The Judge ordered the officer to answer a few more questions, outside the hearing of the jury, concerning the extent to which Johnson's statement had been the result of questioning by the officer, versus the extent to which Johnson's statement had been spontaneous. After argument by both the PD and the DA, Judge Baldwin decided that the statement had been spontaneous, not the result of questions, and that it had not in fact been coerced. Accordingly, *Miranda* did not apply. So, the jury should be able to hear it. Next, there was the issue of the People's failure to tell the PD about the statement before. There, Judge Baldwin found the DA was as surprised as the PD; he also found that the defendant was not prejudiced by the late discovery of the statement, and that at the request of the PD he would continue the trial— that, is, delay the rest of the case—if the PD needed more time to prepare to cross examine the police officers on the statement. So, the judge overruled the objection by the PD. He denied the motion for a mistrial.

The PD replied that he objected to the court's ruling, but didn't need more time to prepare his cross examination.

The judge had the jury brought back in, and the questioning of the police officer continued. The jury had in fact been out for almost an hour, and some of them were impatient and frustrated by the delay. This was especially so since they didn't know why they had been excused from the courtroom. There was not much Judge Baldwin could do about that, except to apologize, and let the jury know that he and the lawyers had been working hard to resolve an important legal issue.

Motion for Acquittal

After the last witness for the People testified, the DA formally "rested" his case. Then the PD rose and said he had a motion; he didn't specify what kind of motion it was, and indeed said nothing else in front of the jury. The judge knew what was coming—a motion for judgment of acquittal—which is a motion that cannot be made, argued, or decided in front of a jury. If a judge denies a motion for judgment of acquittal, the jury may think that the judge is endorsing the People's case, or suggesting the defendant is probably guilty, which would be entirely incorrect because the judge uses an entirely different standard to decide the motion than the jury does to make its decision.

Thus Judge Baldwin once more excused the jury, and heard argument. The PD argued that the People had not proved one of the elements of the crime—that Johnson's blood alcohol level was over 0.08 %. The proof of that, the PD argued, was solely based on the reading of breath analyzer machines, and those had been shown to have serious mechanical issues. No jury could find, *beyond a reasonable doubt,* that those machines were accurate. The DA then argued that the evidence on reliability, and age of equipment, all related to the weight of the evidence. He made this point knowing that judges are not meant, on motions for judgment of acquittal, to *weigh* the evidence, because that is a function for the jury. Judge Baldwin agreed, holding there was enough evidence in the record to allow the jury to consider it, and denied the defense motion.

The jury returned to hear evidence from the defense.

Defendant's Case

Defendants in a criminal case may win without putting on any evidence at all. It is the burden of the People (or the "Government", in a federal criminal case) to prove their case, and if they do not the jury should acquit the defendant. Often the defense indeed puts on no evidence. In this case, the PD called Bob Slader to testify about the traffic light at the time of the accident. The PD also called an expert in field sobriety tests, a retired police officer who testified that in his opinion the tests were worthless. On cross examination it turned out that the officer had retired about 15 years ago, and did not know how field sobriety tests were currently performed.

The PD then rested her case.

Rebuttal

The DA made some frantic calls overnight after the defense rested, and found a police officer who taught at the police academy, and could testify about the basis for field sobriety tests as they are currently done. She asked to meet the officer for breakfast, the next day. At that meeting, the DA learned two things. First, the witness knew a lot, and had the perfect set of experiences to qualify him to rebut what the PD's witness had said. But secondly, the officer would make a terrible witness. His eyes kept shifting and blinking; he never looked her in the eye. He was difficult to understand, and he used words with five syllables instead of simple straightforward English. The DA thought the jury would find him patronizing and unconvincing, and she certainly didn't want to end her case with the memory of this witness, as it were, in the jury's mind as they marched off to the jury deliberation room. She reluctantly thanked the officer for meeting with her, made some excuses, and hurried off to court. She told the Judge that the People had no rebuttal, and was done.

Jury Instructions & Closing Argument

As with civil cases, the judge must instruct the jury on the law as it applies to the case. That includes not only the definition of the crime, and what the jury needs to find is true beyond a reasonable doubt to find the defendant guilty, but also a variety of other instructions that help the jury deliberate. The judge addresses how to evaluate witnesses and their credibility and instructs that the testimony of a single witnesses is (usually) enough to prove any fact. He discusses how to consider the opinions of experts, the definition of "reasonable doubt" and the principle that a defendant is presumed innocent, unless and until the People prove his guilt. He also explains direct and indirect (or "circumstantial") evidence—both are fine in court. He gives instructions on being courteous and open minded during deliberations, and other topics. The lawyers are expected to propose instructions on the first day of trial, and as the trial winds it way to the end, the judge and lawyers meet to discuss which instructions should be given, which the judge will refuse, and which the judge will modify. If they need to communicate with the judge during their deliberations, the jury is told to put their question in writing, and he will either send them a written response or bring them out to open court to instruct them.

As soon as the last witnesses testified, the judge read the jury instructions to the jury, telling them that they would have a copy to review when they retired to deliberate in the jury room.

Both sides gave impassioned closing arguments. The prosecutor (assistant district attorney) went first, followed by the defense counsel. Finally the prosecutor had the last word in "rebuttal" argument, and asked the jury to return a verdict of guilty on all counts.

The bailiff was sworn by the clerk, and she took charge of the jury. Under the bailiff's oath, she would not let anyone communicate with the jury, or they with anyone, while they were in deliberations, except on order of the court.

In a high profile case being covered by the press, the jury will sometimes be *sequestered*, which means they will be guarded twenty-four hours a day by the deputies who work in the Sheriff's office (also knows as bailiffs). In federal court, these duties are handled by the U.S. Marshal's Service. In these high profile cases the state pays for food and lodging while the trial and deliberations are ongoing. But this is very, very rare. Normally, the jury is simply instructed by the judge not to discuss the case with anyone, not to do any research or investigate anything to do with the case, and to avoid all media references about the case when they go home at night or break for meals and such.

Jury Deliberations

The jury deliberated for two days. In a note to the judge, the jury asked for a read-back of the testimony of one of the police officer witnesses, but simply said in their note that they wanted to hear the testimony without specifying which parts of it. The judge sent back another note asking for clarification—did the jury want the entire testimony read back? No, they only wanted the testimony as it related to field sobriety tests. Unfortunately, a quick view of the court reporter's notes showed that the subject was scattered across many parts of the direct and cross examination. During the roughly hour and half it took to get the lawyers back into the courtroom, areas of the testimony isolated to the satisfaction of both lawyers and the judge, and notes prepared, the impatient jury sent out another note asking for the read back. The judge had the jury brought back, and patiently explained to them the steps that were being taken to prepare the court reporter's notes. Later the jury asked to see a PowerPoint exhibit that the DA has used in her closing argument, where she had put up on the screen her "bullet points" outlining her case against Johnson. Unfortunately, as with many items made to demonstrate or illustrate a witness' testimony, the PowerPoint itself had not actually been admitted into evidence, and so the Judge was unable to send it in to the jury. He explained this to them in a written note.

On the second day, the jury sent out a note that they couldn't reach a verdict. That was signed by the presiding juror (or foreperson). Another note also came out, signed by juror number 4, which said that one of the jurors refused to discuss the case further and was causing a lot of problems.

The judge at that point was actually in the middle of selecting a jury for another case. He asked the new panel to take a break—much to their frustration—and had the jury brought into the courtroom. Judge Baldwin first re-read instructions about listening and discussing, about keeping an open mind. He repeated that they must not be afraid to change their minds if they are convinced they are wrong, and not to change their mind just to accommodate others. And he emphasized that they had a duty to deliberate and discuss the case among themselves. He asked the presiding juror if he thought further deliberations, reading instructions, or re-reading part of the transcript might be useful. The presiding juror said perhaps more deliberations might help, and the jury was sent back to the jury room.

Verdict

Late on the second day, the buzzer at the bailiff's desk in the courtroom sounded yet again, surprising everyone in the courtroom. The judge was just finishing a hearing on a motion to suppress on a different case. He asked the lawyers on that case to finish up their questions while the PD and the DA were sent for. The judge decided the motion to suppress, explaining his reasons on the record in open court, picked a next date for a hearing in that case, and dismissed the lawyers. He then turned to the bailiff, directing that the jury be brought in.

The jury had reached a verdict.

The verdict form read 'guilty' and it was so read by the court clerk. The judge asked if any party wished the jury polled. The PD did, and everyone watched the face of each juror as he or she was asked whether the verdict as read was in fact his or her verdict. "Is this your true verdict?" each one was asked. Each answered yes, although juror number 11 paused for a brief second during which everyone in the courtroom held his breath. After the polling, the judge ordered the clerk to record the verdict and formally asked whether the parties wished a re-reading of the verdict as recorded. They declined.

The judge thanked the jury for their service, indicating that he knew they had taken time out of their personal and professional lives to serve this most important function, bringing the wisdom and intelligence of the community to determine important issues of fact which profoundly affect the lives their fellow citizens. He told them that his repeated orders not to discuss the case, or the people, or any of the issues involved in the case, were all now of no effect, and they could talk about the case, and their deliberations, with anyone they chose. The parties, and their lawyers, might now approach them to talk about the case, but the jury should discuss the case only if they so wished, and at a time and place of their choosing. Judge Baldwin then dismissed the jury.

The judge turned to the defendant and, based on the conviction, remanded him into custody with no bail. At this point, he didn't want to take any chances of Johnson fleeing, and after this conviction it was clear that a substantial period of prison time would be ordered at sentencing. The bailiffs took Johnson into their charge, placed handcuffs on him, and led him away. The judge exonerated bail, that is, he cancelled it. He did this because bail was no longer needed to guarantee Johnson's presence for court hearings. Johnson got back the deed and title to his house which he had posted as security for his bail.

The judge ordered a presentence report from the probation office, and set the sentencing for thirty days out.

The verdict had been unanimous. If the vote had been anything other than 12-0 for either 'guilty' or 'not guilty', then the case would have had to have been retried, although of course the DA could have decided to drop the charges instead of a retrial, or the PD and Johnson could have agreed to a deal instead of asking for another trial. For this reason, when a jury is hopelessly deadlocked and cannot come to a unanimous verdict the judge asks them what the vote is, just before discharging them. This information tells the lawyers how close the verdict was—if it were for example 11-1 for guilty, the DA might well want to re-try the case, whereas if it were 6-6 or 9-3 for 'not guilty', then the DA might not retry the case, or might offer a better deal than before to the defendant to resolve the case.

There are many reasons the judge might declare a mistrial, not just because of a failure to reach a unanimous verdict. Any participant in the trial (including the judge) might make a mistake, or indeed commit misconduct, which renders the trial unfair. The judge will try to correct the error if he can by giving various instructions to the jury, but sometimes the problem can not be cured and the jury has to be let go, and the case tried over again. As a general rule, if a case is mistried through no fault of the DA, it can be retried. But if the DA does something to cause the mistrial, the U.S. Constitution's bar on double jeopardy usually blocks a new trial and the charges have to be dismissed.

Sentencing

The case was brought on for sentencing. The judge and counsel had reviewed the recommendation from the probation department. That department had reviewed Johnson's prior criminal history, interviewed him, reviewed the seriousness of the crimes and analyzed other aggravating and mitigating factors. The PD and DA had also filed sentencing memoranda, which the judge had read. Predictably, the DA argued there were no mitigating circumstances, while the PD focused only on those, including Johnson's prior community based work for a local food bank. The PD argued that Johnson's family needed him, that he'd never drink again, and that he was still the subject of the civil suit by Hollings and Pitt. The DA emphasized the fact that Hollings was dead, Pitt permanently disfigured and handicapped, the high blood alcohol content, and that Johnson had shown little remorse, among other things.

The sentencing hearing was difficult, for everyone. The victims spoke. Kim Hollings' mother and father talked about their daughter, and most of the people in court were in tears. Judge Baldwin ordered a five minute recess, and used the opportunity to compose himself as well. The courtroom heard from Pitt, about himself and what it meant to him to lose Kim Hollings. Then Johnson's teenage daughter spoke, about her need for her father, their relationship, how she knew he would never forget what had happened for the rest of his life. She pleaded with the judge to have her father back. "I can't bring back Kim Hollings, your honor," she said, "but the misery doesn't have to destroy everyone. Let my father serve a minimal sentence and release him on probation, and let him do something good and useful on the outside to make up for what happened here."

The room was still. This was very, very difficult for everyone. Johnson finally approached the lectern, his hands and feet shackled, dressed in a bright orange prison garb. Defendants always have the right to be heard at sentencing. At first no one could hear Johnson; he couldn't get the words out. "I can't talk," were the first words heard. He then went on to apologize, promised never to drink again, and stopped. There were other things he had wanted to say, but at this point none of them seemed to matter. He stood, head down, and waited.

In most cases judges have a variety of options. They can sentence someone to county jail for up to a year, to state prison for periods in excess of that, and/or impose time on probation attaching conditions to that probation. Conditions of probation in a DUI case might include taking a offender's counseling program, paying fines and fees, using an ignition interlock device which prevents anyone who has alcohol in his blood from driving, performing community services hours, undergoing various kinds of counseling such as drug and alcohol counseling, anger management, job training, parenting classes etc., whatever the judge thinks might help address some of the underlying reasons for the criminal behavior.

Judge Baldwin reviewed the mitigating and aggravating circumstances. He acknowledged the statements of all who had spoken, and concluded that the facts were as bad as they could be. The legislature, he said, had a maximum sentence in these types of cases of twenty years. With Johnson's prior record for driving while under the influence, the judge concluded, the maximum was the correct sentence. He sentenced Johnson to twenty years in the state prison, and remanded the defendant to the custody of the bailiffs, to be transported to prison. He advised Johnson of his right to appeal, and told him exactly what the deadline was to file his notice of appeal. Johnson was told that if he couldn't afford a lawyer on appeal, one would be provided to him free of charge.

Johnson looked back at his family, and was escorted out of the courtroom. He wouldn't spend all twenty years in prison, because if he had good behavior he'd be released on parole before that. But he'd not see his little girl grow up. His wife probably would divorce him, and he'd lose everything else. Hollings was dead, Pitt crippled for life. This was a case of many, many tragedies.

These cases end up in the courts, but often the courts cannot really fix anything. They act to punish, to deter similar actions by others, to keep dangerous criminals off the streets, and to provide some rough sense that malefactors are accountable for their actions.

But judges cannot "unring the bell," and they cannot bring back the past.

Appeals

Johnson appealed his judgment of conviction. Because he had been tried in the San Francisco Superior Court, his case went to the First District Court of Appeal which governs San Francisco, Marin, Alameda, and some of the neighboring counties in California. The First District Court of Appeal happens to have its courthouse in San Francisco. The appellate court had no choice but to hear the appeal. The trial transcript was prepared, at state expense, so that the court of appeal would be able to see exactly what everyone had said, from the moment of jury selection all the way through to the last words at sentencing.

The case on appeal was actually handled by a different set of lawyers, ones who had substantial experience in appellate litigation, which calls for skills somewhat different from those used at trial. Many lawyers who regularly appear in courts of appeal specialize in that sort of work. Also, having a different sets of lawyers on appeal can bring fresh and more objective set of eyes to the case. The Public Defender's office has specialists in this work, and the office of the Attorney General often handles appeals for DAs around the state.

The court of appeal set out a briefing schedule, with Johnson's lawyer going first with his opening brief. The Attorney General filed an opposition brief, and the PD's office filed a final reply brief. After oral argument, the court of appeal concluded that the trial had been fair, any errors were harmless (they made no difference to the outcome), and the judge below in the Superior Court had properly exercised his discretion when it came to sentencing. The court of appeal pointed out that while it might not have made the same decisions made by Judge Baldwin, the appellate court was not going to substitute its judgment for his where it was clear he had decided within the acceptable range of his discretion. The three judge panel discussed this in the context of one particular decision made by Judge Baldwin, which was his decision that Johnson's prior shoplifting conviction would be admissible if Johnson took the stand, because it reflected on his veracity as a witness. The shoplifting case was about six years old at the time of Johnson's trial, and Johnson's lawyer had objected to the jury's hearing about the old conviction. The PD had told Judge Baldwin on the record that if the prior conviction were going to be let in, he'd keep Johnson off the witness stand and Johnson would not testify in his own defense. But Judge Baldwin had expressly weighed the competing considerations. The issue was within his discretion, and the court of appeal saw that he had in fact exercised his discretion, as opposed to making an arbitrary ruling.

The conviction was affirmed.

The PD's office filed a petition for certiorari to the state Supreme Court. Arguments were made in that petition that issues of statewide concern were at stake. The California Supreme Court apparently thought no statewide or more general issues were at stake, nor that the law needed clarification, and it denied the cert. petition in a one-line order.

The PD could then have asked the U.S. Supreme Court in Washington, D.C. to take the case, by filing a petition for certiorari in that court. But there was no substantial federal question they could think of which might tempt that federal court to take the case, and they didn't bother with the futile effort.

Time expired for the U.S. Supreme Court review. The case was sent back to the superior court; the judgment was final, and appeals were exhausted. Johnson served out his sentence.

Revocation of Probation

Johnson's sentence might have included a period of probation; many sentences do. Sometimes defendants serve some time in custody as a condition of their probation. Sometimes, they are simply placed on a period of probation for, say, three or five years. There are always conditions to probation, such as undergoing counseling, paying fines, staying away from certain people or neighborhoods, carrying no weapons, making restitution to the victims, and so on. One condition for every probationary period is, "You shall violate no laws." Therefore, if someone on probation violates the law again he then faces *two* cases- the new charges he was just arrested for, and a motion by the DA to *revoke* his old probation. Assume Johnson had received the (unlikely!) sentence of probation for five years with the condition he serve six months in the county jail. After his release from jail, he'd be on probation-- and assume he then was arrested for assault, shoplifting, or any other crime. He would have to stand trial for the new charge, and the People would ask that his probation on his old case be revoked.

In a hearing to revoke probation, there is no jury. The judge simply hears evidence and then decides whether or not the defendant has again violated the law (or violated any other condition of probation), and if so, the judge can then sentence the defendant on the old crime to the maximum time in jail and up to the maximum fine for that old crime. In addition to that, the defendant may be convicted by the jury of the new charge, too. If that happens, he also can be sentenced on the new crime.

Probation can be revoked for the violation of *any* of the conditions, not just that one which requires him to stay crime free. So if the probationer fails to report as ordered to his probation officer, or is found in a neighborhood which was barred to him, of fails to attend anger management classes as ordered, he can be sentenced up to the maximum sentence for his old crime. The judge also can put him back on probation, and/or change the conditions of probation. All of these decisions are within the discretion of the trial judge.

Conclusion

The stories presented in this book are just that—stories. They include bits and pieces from many cases, and some invented incidents. We purposefully plotted stories that resulted in a conviction in the criminal case, because we wanted to illustrate the appeals process. Not all cases result in convictions; in many situations the jury (or the judge, if it is a bench trial) issues a 'not guilty' verdict, and the defendant is immediately freed. We plotted a civil case in which the plaintiff won, for the same purpose: so we could illustrate the entire process of a case. Many civil cases result in a defense verdict, where for example the judge grants a motion for summary judgment, or directs a verdict for the defense, or the jury finds for the defense. Of course, as the reader now knows, most cases actually settle without resort to the entire process mapped out in this book.

The stories here are not realistic for another reason. As the reader will now understand, a criminal case will very likely happen before a civil case based on the same facts: you will recall this is because the defendant in a criminal case has a right to a *speedy trial*; and civil cases often take a year or two (or more) to prepare for trial. When a defendant like Johnson in our case loses the criminal trial, a legal doctrine called *res judicata* (pronounced "race ju-di-ca-ta") will in effect transfer the finding of responsibility (or "liability") from the criminal case to the civil case. Parties in the civil case won't have to prove, all over again, the fact that Johnson is legally responsible for the car crash and the death of Hollings. Because of this legal doctrine, it is actually unlikely that there would have been a civil case at all; at least, it probably would have settled before trial.

Too, many cases are more complicated than those described here. In the civil case, for example, Hollings and Pitt might have sued Ed, the "friendly" bartender, as well as Johnson. They would have done this if they thought they could prove that Ed must have known Johnson was in no shape to drive. And Ed then might then have sued Johnson. Johnson might have sued Ed, too, e.g., for serving him too much alcohol. In both the civil case and criminal cases, the parties used expert witnesses to testify about matters that are outside most people's usual range of knowledge; we did not discuss how lawyers choose and prepare experts. And more generally our stories did not describe most of the time consuming and expensive out-of-court research and investigation that lawyers do to prepare for various hearings and trial.

But despite the liberties we have taken, all the events portrayed do happen in a variety of cases, and usually in the order portrayed. The reader has a sense of what judges and juries do, as well as the other major participants in a trial. We hope that many of the mysteries of jury selection, evidentiary objections, and appeals, have been dispelled. Above all, we hope that the reader understands how the U.S. Constitution (and its state counterparts) actually manifests in the judicial system: how constitutional guarantees are enforced, how the three branches of government come together in the courtroom, how the final results of a trial come from the citizens of this Nation, sitting as juries, under the supervision of a judge who has taken an oath to uphold the Constitution.

The American judicial system is a powerful guarantor of fairness, transparency, and accountability on the part of people as well as their government. It is the foundation of our faith in our government. But it is also a delicate creation: it is as good and honest as the people who work within its confines, and it entirely depends on a public that understands and treasures its principles. We hope that this book will further that understanding.

About the Authors

Marilyn Englander received her bachelor's degree from Harvard University, where she met co-author Curtis Karnow. She went on to complete an interdisciplinary PhD in history, anthropology and religious studies at University of California, Santa Barbara. After 25 years of teaching humanities courses at middle school through university-level, she established her own school, REAL School Marin, in Marin County, California. Her teenage students focus on personal and civic responsibility as well as global citizenship through studying American history, government and conflict resolution.

Curtis Karnow is a judge on the San Francisco Superior Court. He is the author of FUTURE CODES: ESSAYS IN ADVANCED COMPUTER TECHNOLOGY AND THE LAW (Artech House), contributory co-author of E-BUSINESS AND INSURANCE (CCH) (chapters on Internet security, copyright, trademarks and trade dress, indirect liability on the internet), INTERNATIONAL E-COMMERCE (CCH) (privacy & security), NETWORK SECURITY: THE COMPLETE REFERENCE (McGraw-Hill), and CYBERCRIME: DIGITAL COPS IN A NETWORKED ENVIRONMENT (NYU Press). He is consulting editor on ACTION GUIDE: HANDLING EXPERT WITNESSES IN CALIFORNIA COURTS (CEB); and CALIFORNIA CIVIL DISCOVERY PRACTICE (CEB). Topics of his law review articles range from artificial intelligence to summary judgment and game theory. Judge Karnow is married to the other author of this book, and together they have two children, Benjamin and Jean.

Appendices

142

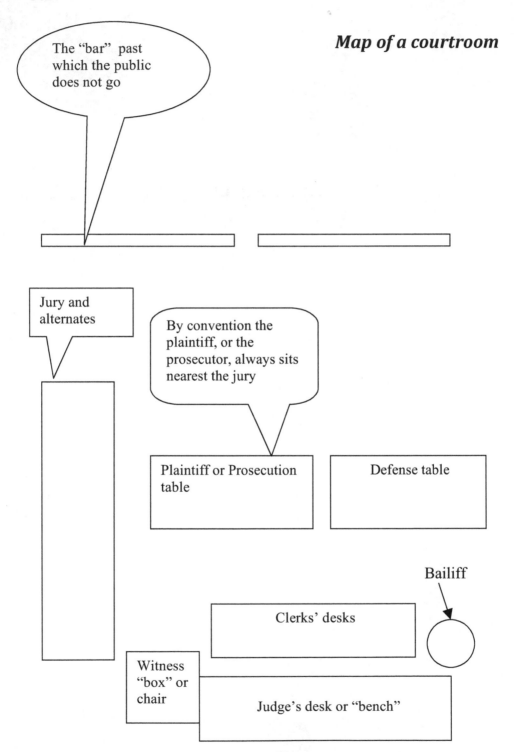

Map of a courtroom

Federal court system

(With thanks for extracts from The Administrative Office of the U.S. Courts, http://www.uscourts.gov/faq.html)

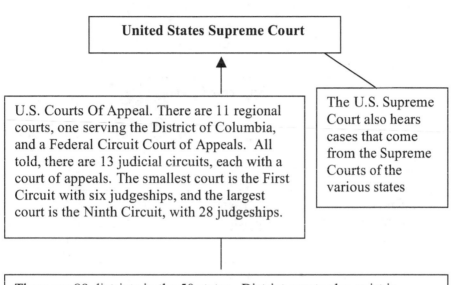

United States Supreme Court

U.S. Courts Of Appeal. There are 11 regional courts, one serving the District of Columbia, and a Federal Circuit Court of Appeals. All told, there are 13 judicial circuits, each with a court of appeals. The smallest court is the First Circuit with six judgeships, and the largest court is the Ninth Circuit, with 28 judgeships.

The U.S. Supreme Court also hears cases that come from the Supreme Courts of the various states

There are 89 districts in the 50 states. District courts also exist in Puerto Rico, the Virgin Islands, the District of Columbia, Guam, and the Northern Mariana Islands. In total there are 94 U.S. district courts. Some states, such as Alaska, are composed of a single judicial district. Others, such as California, are composed of multiple judicial districts.

California state court system

California Supreme Court

↑

District Courts of Appeal. There are six of these appellate courts, and each generally covers many counties

↑

Superior Courts. There is one Superior Court for each of the state's 58 counties. Some counties have a few judges, others such as Los Angeles County have hundreds of judges. A county may have one or many courthouses.

Sample criminal code excerpts

Below, we provide a part of California's Penal Code. This Code is the series of statutes enacted by the Legislature which define crimes and specify the maximum punishment for each crime. The entire Penal Code is over 1300 pages of very small print. In fact, many crimes are defined, and the punishment is set, in other codes as well, such as California's Health and Safety Code (drug related offenses), Business and Profession Code (crimes by professions and some businesses), and the Vehicle Code (such as drunk driving and speeding), among others. As you briefly review the extract from the Penal Code below, note that the crime is defined, and the punishment is set. The punishment varies, depending on what kind of person is the subject of the crime. Note how the statute defines the words it uses.

PENAL CODE SECTION 240-248

240. An assault is an unlawful attempt, coupled with a present ability, to commit a violent injury on the person of another.

241. (a) An assault is punishable by a fine not exceeding one thousand dollars ($1,000), or by imprisonment in the county jail not exceeding six months, or by both the fine and imprisonment.

(b) When an assault is committed against the person of a parking control officer engaged in the performance of his or her duties, and the person committing the offense knows or reasonably should know that the victim is a parking control officer, the assault is punishable by a fine not exceeding two thousand dollars ($2,000), or by imprisonment in the county jail not exceeding six months, or by both the fine and imprisonment.

(c) When an assault is committed against the person of a peace officer, firefighter, emergency medical technician, mobile intensive care paramedic, lifeguard, process server, traffic officer, code enforcement officer, or animal control officer engaged in the performance of his or her duties, or a physician or nurse engaged in rendering emergency medical care outside a hospital, clinic, or other health care facility, and the person committing the offense knows or reasonably should know that the victim is a peace officer, firefighter, emergency medical technician, mobile intensive care paramedic, lifeguard, process server, traffic officer, code enforcement officer, or animal control officer engaged in the performance of his or her duties, or a physician or nurse engaged in rendering emergency medical care, the assault is punishable by a fine not exceeding two thousand dollars ($2,000), or by imprisonment in the county jail not exceeding one year, or by both the fine and imprisonment.

(d) As used in this section, the following definitions apply:

(1) Peace officer means any person defined in Chapter 4.5 (commencing with Section 830) of Title 3 of Part 2.

(2) "Emergency medical technician" means a person possessing a valid course completion certificate from a program approved by the State Department of Health Services for the medical training and education of ambulance personnel, and who meets the standards of Division 2.5 (commencing with Section 1797) of the Health and safety Code.

(3) "Mobile intensive care paramedic" refers to those persons who meet the standards set forth in Division 2.5 (commencing with section 1797) of the Health and Safety Code.

(4) "Nurse" means a person who meets the standards of Division 2.5 (commencing with Section 1797) of the Health and Safety Code.

(5) "Lifeguard" means a person who is:

(A) Employed as a lifeguard by the state, a county, or a city, and is designated by local ordinance as a public officer who has a duty and responsibility to enforce local ordinances and misdemeanors through the issuance of citations.

(B) Wearing distinctive clothing which includes written identification of the person's status as a lifeguard and which clearly identifies the employing organization.

(6) "Process server" means any person who meets the standards or is expressly exempt from the standards set forth in Section 22350 of the Business and Professions Code.

(7) "Traffic officer" means any person employed by a county or city to monitor and enforce state laws and local ordinances relating to parking and the operation of vehicles.

(8) "Animal control officer" means any person employed by a county or city for purposes of enforcing animal control laws or regulations.

(9) (A) "Code enforcement officer" means any person who is not described in Chapter 4.5 (commencing with Section 830) of Title 3 of Part 2 and who is employed by any governmental subdivision, public or quasi-public corporation, public agency, public service corporation, any town, city, county, or municipal corporation, whether incorporated or chartered, that has enforcement authority for health, safety, and welfare requirements, and whose duties include enforcement of any statute, rules, regulations, or standards, and who is authorized to issue citations, or file formal complaints.

(B) "Code enforcement officer" also includes any person who is employed by the Department of Housing and Community Development who has enforcement authority for health, safety, and welfare requirements pursuant to the Employee Housing Act (Part 1 (commencing with Section 17000) of Division 13 of the Health and Safety Code); the State Housing Law (Part 1.5 (commencing with Section 17910) of Division 13 of the Health and Safety Code); the Mobilehomes-Manufactured Housing Act (Part 2 (commencing with Section 18000) of Division 13 of the Health and Safety Code); the Mobilehome Parks Act (Part 2.1 (commencing with Section 18200) of Division 13 of the Health and Safety Code); and the Special Occupancy Parks Act (Part 2.3 (commencing with Section 18860) of Division 13 of the Health and Safety Code).

(10) "Parking control officer" means any person employed by a city, county, or city and county, to monitor and enforce state laws and local ordinances relating to parking.

Sample court memorandum & order

This is a real memorandum and order issued in a criminal case, with a few things (such as the name) changed. (This decision may have been reversed by an appellate court—do not read this as an authoritative application of the law!) This provides a sense of what these sorts of documents look like. The issue in this case was whether the defendant's speedy trial rights had been violated. Those rights are guaranteed by the U.S. (federal) Constitution, as well as by state law. Here, the Court weighed various factors and applied a test set out by the U.S. Supreme Court (in a case called *Barker v. Wingo*) and concluded that the right to a speedy trial had been violated. For that reason the Court dismissed the charges.

SUPERIOR COURT OF CALIFORNIA
COUNTY OF ZZZ

People of the State of California, *Plaintiff,* vs. *xxxxx[Defendant],* *Defendant.*	*CASE NO: 06-1111* *ORDER GRANTING* *MOTION TO DISMISS* *FOR VIOLATION OF* *RIGHT TO SPEEDY* *TRIAL*

Defendant moves for dismissal of the charges based on the delay in his arraignment. He was arrested May 9, 2005, and a complaint was filed May 11, 2005. Despite suggestions to the contrary in defendant's papers, he was served with and signed a citation on or about May 9, 2005, which required him to appear in court May 12, 2005. As he states, he was in custody for some days after his arrest, and indeed the file shows a probable cause determination May 10, 2005. Court computer files suggest he was released at about 10.34 p.m. the night of May 11, that is, the evening before he was to appear.

The defendant failed to appear at his court hearing, and a bench warrant issued. He states he learned of the outstanding warrant at the beginning of 2006. He added himself to calendar to resolve the matter on

January 10, 2006, and was arraigned January 19, 2006. He cites the delay between May 2005 and his January 2006 arraignment as the basis for his motion.

The central factors in the motion are famously set forth in *Barker v. Wingo*, 407 US 514 (1972): the length of the delay, the reason for it, defendant's assertion of his right, and prejudice to the defendant. As a matter of state law, only actual prejudice and the reasons for the delay need be considered. Fundamentally, the question involves weighing factors designed to attribute the fault for the delay to either the People or the defendant.

The reason for the delay was defendant's failure to appear when ordered. His declaration in support of the motion contends that he thought the charges had been dropped, but no specific basis for this belief is set forth,[1] and defendant alludes to no basis created by, or the fault of, the state. The very purpose of the formal citation process is to have a record of the command to appear. The defendant's signature appears on the citation. The issue here is whether defendant's belief that (a) there was no such order, or (b) that the order was in some fashion ineffective is entitled to any weight.

As it happens the defendant's state of mind when he failed to appear *is* material: apparently the delay will not be charged to him if he was ignorant of the need to appear. *Ogle v. Superior Court*, 4 Cal. App. 4th 1007, 1019, 1021 (1992). On the one hand, based on "the original citation bearing [defendant's] signed promise to appear, [the Court may infer] he willfully and knowingly failed to appear." *Ogle v. Superior Court*, 4 Cal. App. 4th 1007, 1020 (1992). On the other hand, here defendant has provided evidence to confound this: he provided a declaration that he did not know he was to appear, and his actions after May 2005 tend to bear that out: he turned himself in when he was told by an officer that the warrant was pending, and he made no effort to avoid service of process. The timing of his release, too, late at night the day before he was due in court, supports his contentions.

I note that there is no showing of any effort on the part of the People to serve the warrant, although it appears the defendant was not avoiding service and was receiving state benefits under his own name.

---

[1] Supplemental papers filed by defendant include materials suggesting defendant was under the influence of drugs, and also includes materials describing the possible effects of the intoxication. None of that material is in admissible form and I ignore it.

There is some showing of prejudice. The claim is that an unidentified person was at the scene of the alleged offense and might corroborate a defense. The defendant claims that as of last May he had known the person for two months and could then have located him, but now he has forgotten the name of the person; his efforts to locate him now are limited to standing at the street intersection where the alleged crime took place, suggesting that the defendant did not know the address of this person. It is thus difficult to conclude that the unknown person would have been located last May. This weakens the showing of prejudice.

Accordingly I am left with a moderate (in the context of this misdemeanor case) delay of eight months, a weak showing of prejudice, no effort on the part of the People to bring the case to trial, and by the preponderance of the evidence a showing that the delay was not attributable to defendant's willful and intentional act in failing to appear. Under these circumstances, the balance of the factors weighs in defendant's favor.

The motion to dismiss is granted.

Dated: March x, 2006   _____[signed]_____
                                          Judge of the Superior Court

Sample court minutes of a sentencing

Superior Court of California, County of San Francisco

People of the State of California v. J.J.		
	Assistant DA: Mary Roe	Attorney of Record: John Doe
Interpreter:	Clerk: D.V.	Judge: XYZ
Reporter: L.P.		

Cause on Calendar for: sentencing

Count	Code	Section MC#	Plea	Finding
1	PC	459/m	NG	NG
2	PC	666/m	NG	G
3	PC	148(a)/m	NG	G

DA Angela Bean appeared for today's calling

The People and The defense file their sentencing recommendations

Time is waived for sentencing.
The court orders imposition of sentence suspended.
The probation ordered shall be served as unsupervised probation (court probation).
Probation is ordered granted for a period of three years subject to the following terms and conditions:
As a condition of probation the defendant shall serve a term in County Jail of 30 days.
Defendant is to receive credit for time served of 4 days.
Sentence may be served through SWAP. Defendant is ordered to report April 2, 2008 at 8: a.m. and pay SWAP fees as determined.
Defendant is subject to warrantless search condition, as to defendant's person, property, premises and vehicle, at any time of the day or night, with or without probable cause, by any peace, parole, or probation officer.
Defendant is OR'd to SWAP.
Defendant shall pay a court security fee in the amount of $20.
Defendant shall pay a restitution fine in the amount of $100 pursuant to PC 1202.4(b).
Defendant shall obey all laws.
Defendant accepts conditions of probation.
The sentences on count 2 & 3 are concurrent.

Dept: 003 Date: 3/29/08
Attest: D.V. , Deputy Clerk

Explanation of Minutes

Reproduced on the last page is a page of "minutes". These are the official records of what happens in court. You can usually view these in publicly accessible files of the case. On this sample, we see the events that took place when a defendant, Mr JJ, was sentenced by the judge. At the top, we have the record of who was in the courtroom at the time, and the lawyers involved. We see below that information that the defendant was charged with three counts, i.e., three different crimes. He originally entered a plea of "Not Guilty" (NG) to each of these. He was found guilty (G) of two of those crimes-- a violation of PC (Penal Code) 666, which is a petty theft having previously been convicted of a similar crime, and a violation of PC 148, which is interfering with a police officer. The indication after the code section—"/m"—indicates that all these crimes are misdemeanors, and not the more serious type of crime, felonies. Judge XYZ sentenced Mr. JJ to serve three years of probation. But as conditions of that probation, JJ had to serve 30 days in custody, with credit for 4 days he had already served in jail-- i.e. 26 days. Instead of having to serve that 26 days in jail, the judge has decided he is eligible for the Sheriff's Work Alternative Program (SWAP), and he was released on his own recognizance (no bail needed— "OR'd") so he could report to SWAP. He has to pay some fees and fines, and for the three years he's on probation he (and his car, and home, etc.) can be searched at any time for no reason. Mr. JJ got the same sentence on both of the two counts he was convicted of.

Resources

Anthony Lewis, GIDEON'S TRUMPET (2d ed. Vintage Press: 1968). A superb story of the case which went all the way to the U.S. Supreme Court, ending with a decision which endorsed the Sixth Amendment's guarantee of a lawyer even for those criminal defendants who can not afford the fees.

Anthony Lewis, FREEDOM FOR THE THOUGHT THAT WE HATE: A BIOGRAPHY OF THE FIRST AMENDMENT (2008). This wonderful and relatively short book traces the history and meaning of the First Amendment.

Benjamin Cardozo, THE NATURE OF THE JUDICIAL PROCESS (1921). A classic series of essays on what judges do, written by one of the greatest judges of the last century. Available at http://xroads.virginia.edu/~HYPER/CARDOZO/CarNat.html as well as at http://www.constitution.org/cmt/cardozo/jud_proc.htm

Richard Posner, HOW JUDGES THINK (2008). This is one view, by an eminent federal appellate judge, of the process of, and influences on, judging.

The 1999 Study: "How The Public Views The State Courts," (National Center for State Courts, presented May 14, 1999).

A wonderful movie about a jury is the classic *Twelve Angry Men,* starring Henry Fonda. Another of the authors' favorite movies is *A Man For All Seasons*, a somewhat fictionalized but beautifully written account of Sir Thomas Moore's confrontations with truth, justice, conscience, and the law.

Online:

U.S. Supreme Court. See the opinions filed by the Court, the legal briefs filed by the lawyers, read transcripts of oral arguments, and much more information about the Court: http://www.supremecourtus.gov/

The California Judicial system. Obtain links to most of the courts in the state, read opinions of the Supreme Court, review information about the Judicial Council: http://www.courtinfo.ca.gov/

The federal judicial system:
http://www.fjc.gov/public/home.nsf/autoframe?openform&url_r=pages/
196 . See also http://www.uscourts.gov/

The U.S. Constitution Online: http://www.usconstitution.net/

All California statutes: http://www.leginfo.ca.gov/calaw.html

California's "self help" services for people acting without a lawyer in court
proceedings: http://www.courtinfo.ca.gov/selfhelp/. Most Superior
Courts have their own self help centers as well, both online and in the
courthouse.

The National Association of State Courts has a series of projects,
information, and recommendations on court and attorney outreach to the
community. See e.g.,
http://www.ncsconline.org/D_Research/projects.html#Public%20Trust.

Lawyers referral from the California state bar:
http://www.calbar.ca.gov/state/calbar/calbar_generic.jsp?cid=10182.
Most state bars have lawyer referral services, and indeed even local bars
associated with a specific county or city have their own programs to enable
clients to find lawyers. E.g., http://www.sfbar.org/ (San Francisco Bar
Association)

The American Bar Association: http://www.abanet.org/ This includes
links to a variety of resources for the general public including how to find a
lawyer, and plain English discussions on a variety of legal topics.